After All…

A memoir

by Maria Trautman

Copyright

A Note to Readers

After all ... is a true account of the author's life. To protect the privacy of some individuals the names of all but my closest friends and relatives have been changed. The use of names that are the same as real persons is pure coinciden

Dedication

I dedicate this book first and foremost to my grandmother who was always present in my formative years and who contributed with her wisdom and love, to the person I am today.

I also send it out to all the abused children of the world with my love. I wish I could rescue each and every one of you and offer you the life you deserve, without tears and helplessness. May you find courage to live through your challenges and know that God loves you and will never desert you.

To everyone else … whatever life brings your way, take it as a lesson and carry on with persistence and hope that better things lie ahead. It was with much difficulty that I overcame my past but I am so thankful for the outcome. I am happy, I am loved, I am where I belong. My life is full, I have no regrets.

Sometimes you have to get out of your
body and hide in the deepest recesses
of your mind to survive the chaos.
You have to believe that no matter
how horrible your days are and how
much suffering you're going through,
you will do more than simply survive.
You will thrive, in spite of it all.

Part One

Portugal

Chapter One

Childhood

Grandma and I stood outside our little house in the village of Granja, while the car that carried my mother sped away in a cloud of dust. I didn't know if Grandma was sad to see her go but I could hardly contain my tears. I didn't want Grandma to see me cry because I didn't want her to know how sad I was.

Our little house in the village of Granja was one of the poorest. We had only one bedroom where my grandparents slept and beside it was a small space where a blanket covered the floor, and that's where I slept. The tiny kitchen had a fireplace where Grandma cooked our meals in the three-legged iron pot. We didn't have a chimney so the smoke from the fire exited the house through holes in the broken ceiling tiles. When my mother or aunt visited, and that wasn't very often, they only stayed for the day because we couldn't accommodate them overnight.

My mother had come to visit with Aunt Licinia but she hardly looked at me and when she did, I saw nothing but disdain on her face.

I thought my mother was beautiful. The way she walked, the relaxed way she laughed with my aunt, and her hair. Her hair was done so nice, with shiny combs like I had never seen before. I thought she could be a princess, all she needed was the beautiful long dress. I wanted so much for her to love me. I couldn't remember the last time she came from the city to visit my grandmother but I knew I always waited to see her with anticipation. Maybe this time she would show some interest in me, maybe she would touch me or even kiss me, but my longing for these things was always crushed. Always the same: she ignored me and wanted nothing to do with me.

I watched the cloud of dust disappear down the road and then I ran into the house. I looked for a hiding place and settled behind the bed in my grandparents' bedroom. I scrunched down and made myself as small as I could, covering my head with my hands and letting out my disappointment and sadness through my tears. I didn't want Grandma to see me cry. She loved me so much, unlike my mother, and I didn't want her to think I wasn't happy with her and wanted my mother instead. I cried heartbreaking tears and at some point, I didn't care who heard me.

"Where are you, my love?" Grandma called out when she got

back in the house.

I held my sobs, hoping Grandma would go back outside.

"I know you're here, come out to Grandma."

"I don't want to." I said, sobbing louder than I intended.

"What's the matter, sweetheart? Why are you crying?" Grandma said when she found me and took me in her arms. Her embrace felt so comforting, her love for me so sweet, but I wanted my mother.

"I'm hungry, Grandma." I lied. She hugged me tighter and whispered, "Shhhhh, don't cry, my love, I will get something for us to eat, come.

I was only five years old but this moment in time has stayed with me as the most precious memory of the only mother I ever had, my grandma.

Now, I am eight years old and for the first time in my life, I'm living with my mother in Lisbon. She had left me with my grandparents as a baby, so she could go to the city and seek her future. My grandmother died shortly after I turned eight and now, I find myself in a stranger's home, where I am ignored and treated as if I am dirty and not worthy of love or attention. I don't ask for anything. I just wish my mother would acknowledge me as her child and treat me as such. But she doesn't.

On this evening, shortly after my grandfather brought me to my mother's home, I sat quietly at the table and watched my stepfather playing with their new baby girl while Mother served dinner. I hated the man. I hated the baby, too. I even hated my mother. But most of all I hated the fact that their dinner, as usual, looked and smelled wonderful, while mine was cold leftover fish taken from the back of the fridge and thrown on a plate. The garbage can was where that fish deserved to go but in my mother's home, I was the garbage disposal.

As I watched her set my stepfather's plate in front of him, my mouth watered. The perfectly fried steak sat on his plate, accompanied by slices of boiled potatoes and dark green rappini. He passed the baby to my mother who laid her down on a blanket on the kitchen floor and then he turned to his meal. My mother then sat beside him and the food before her looked just as appetizing, while mine looked and smelled rotten. I didn't complain though, I never complained.

While they laughed and cooed with the baby, I sat looking at my dinner, saddened at the thought that my mother didn't think me worthy of sharing their food. Head bowed, the tears silently fell on to my plate, but no one noticed. It was as if I wasn't even there.

After dinner they took the baby and went to the living room for fruit and cheese, while I stayed in the kitchen sobbing and wishing I could get away from this place. But where would I go? Grandma was dead and no one in the world cared about me.

The food they didn't finish, my mother took with her to the living room to put in the fridge she kept there, leaving me with a table full of dirty dishes and the smelly fish in front of me.

After a while I got up from the table, took my plate and dumped the food in the garbage. I covered it up with whatever was already in the can so my mother would think I had eaten it all. I was cleaning up and doing the dishes when I heard her rushed footsteps in the hallway. I didn't know what she was up to but the urgency of the sound told me it wasn't good news. She barged into the kitchen and seeing my plate gone from the table, came up to my face and snapped, "What did you do with the fish, you good-for-nothing bitch?"

This woman hated me and I knew it. I had hardly left the house in the month I had been living there and I had no one to turn to.

"I'm sorry but I… it was rotten, so I threw it out." I couldn't hide the tremor in my voice, the tears starting again.

She grabbed my arm and pushed me onto the chair. If she had missed, I'd be lying flat on my back or worse.

"I'll show you, you rotten stupid cow." She walked over to the garbage can and opened the lid, digging the fish out with her hand and slapping it back on the plate. She sat and watched me.

I felt like yelling: My name is Maria de Lourdes, or have you forgotten?

"Eat it." she shouted. I kept my head down but I could feel the rage in her voice.

I looked at the messy fish and bile rose in my throat. "I'm not hungry, I ate some. Please don't make me eat anymore, I'm full." I tried to sound confident. As I looked up at her and sensed her resolve, tears spilled down my face. "I don't want to eat anymore."

"Eat the damn food. I don't have all night to sit here with you." She pointed at the plate with tight lips and fury in her eyes.

I picked at the fish and hesitantly put the first bite in my mouth. I gagged but I knew better than to throw up. I swallowed the fish, bite by torturous bite and when I finished, I sat up straight and stared at her perhaps with a little too much defiance in my gaze and thinking I was going to be sick. She didn't say another word but acknowledged my stare with a look I took for disgust. She got up and sauntered into the living room to join her family. Moments later, I heard laughter mixing with the baby's babble and as my stomach rebelled, I ran to the corner of the room and dropped to my knees before the stone toilet.

Sitting on the cold floor after relieving myself of the horrible food, my thoughts went to the time when I lived with Grandma and Grandpa in Granja. There, I longed for my mother and often wondered about my father, too, but now that I had no one to care for me or about me, my thoughts went back to him.

Was there a chance he might one day come for me? That by some miracle he would appear at our door and claim me as his beloved child? He was my one hope of ever getting out of this hell but in my heart of hearts, I doubted that would ever happen.

My mother's sister, Aunt Licinia, visited us often in the village and when I turned seven and was able to understand my situation, I became curious about where I came from. Knowing that my aunt loved me and I could ask her anything, I would often ask about my father. She once told me that my father had gone to Brazil shortly after I was born.

"Your mother didn't always get along with your grandfather," my aunt told me. "One day after she turned seventeen, she went looking for work in order to get away from him. She ended up in Joao Durao, in your father's house. Afonso and his wife were both teachers and needed a housekeeper and maid for their two young children. They were a respected family in the community but after he got your mother pregnant and his wife found out, your mother was expelled from their house. Shortly after that, your father and his family left for Brazil."

Brazil. From that moment on, the word lived in my imagination. I imagined Brazil to be another small village much like ours and I thought there must be a grand house there, too, and that's where my father lived.

"He didn't want me." I said to my aunt, sadness and desolation taking over my spirit. "My mother didn't want me either, did she? She still doesn't."

"Your mother was barely eighteen and very naïve but obstinate at the same time. She couldn't stay here and didn't want to be tied down with a child, that's why she left you and went to Lisbon."

Chapter Two

Alone

The house was now silent. I came out of my reverie and realized I had cleaned the dishes and tidied up the kitchen. With a heavy heart and soul, I pushed myself up from the table and slipped into the tiny room assigned to me, next to the kitchen. It had been a month since Grandpa brought me here to live with my mother. He left a couple of days after we got here and I knew he didn't want to leave me but he said he was too old to take care of a little girl.

In the night, my memories flared up into nightmares and most of them were about the reason I found myself in this predicament. I missed my grandparents and my simple life in the village. In Lisbon I had no friends. I never went out because my mother was ashamed to be seen with me and most of the time I lived in lonely sadness.

My vivid nightmare that night took me to the day my grandmother could not get up from her bed. I had come home from school and looked into her bedroom when I didn't see her in the kitchen, cooking dinner in the three-legged iron pot over the fire. She slept, so I went back to the kitchen and sat on my little stool, wondering if I should wake her.

A little later, sounds from the bedroom roused me from my thoughts and I recognized the soft voice of my grandma, calling my name. I ran to her room and climbed into the bed beside her, looking into her sad eyes.

"Are you feeling better, Grandma?"

She smiled weakly and seemed to focus her energy so she could speak. "No, I don't feel any better, my darling child. Listen to me." She whispered in a tired voice, barely audible. "You have to be a good girl for Grandpa and help him, because he's going to need you when I'm not here anymore."

"Where are you going, Grandma?" I asked, worried.

"I'm going away, my darling."

"Can I come with you? Please, Grandma?"

She didn't answer but raised her hand off the bed and stroked my head, smiling weakly. When she closed her eyes, I thought she was just tired, so I laid my head on the bed beside her. I loved my grandma so much. I thought maybe I could bring her some comfort by being close to her.

I fell asleep that way, with my head next to hers. When I woke up some time later, I studied her face. She seemed to be sleeping but I sensed there was something wrong.

"Grandma, are you sleeping?" I whispered. There was no

response. "Grandma, wake up." I repeated, shaking her arm. Still she said nothing. I panicked and started to cry.

Having no idea what to do, I ran to cousin Filomena's house on the other side of the village and she rushed back with me. After looking in on Grandma and putting the old mirror in front of Grandma's mouth, she told me my grandma had died.

"Died?" I knew animals died but I had never seen a dead person.

Filomena knelt in front of me and put her hands on my shoulders. "Yes, my dear. She's gone. She's in heaven now."

I was stunned. "Gone? But she's in the bedroom."

"Her soul is gone. She's with God now."

"How could my Grandma go to God without telling me?" I cried. "When is she coming back?"

"Shh, little one," Filomena said, hugging me tight, "Shh."

The next day someone brought a coffin. Two women sat on Grandma's knees so they could lay her straight in it. She had been sleeping on her side with her knees bent when she died. All that day, Grandma lay in the coffin in the middle of our entryway and people came to visit. Grandpa sat beside Grandma's coffin, crying all the time. Sometimes he stopped for a little break but as soon as the next person came in, he started all over again. I had never seen him cry before so I climbed onto his lap and rested my head on his chest, hoping to comfort him.

The following day when I went to school, Miss Alcina hugged me and told me she was sorry that Grandma had died.

"She's gone to be with God," I said sadly.

When I got home that day, Grandpa told me he had to take me to Lisbon to live with my mother and her family.

"But why, Grandpa? Can't I just stay here with you? Grandma

said I should look after you when she was gone. Don't you want me to stay?"

"Yes, I would love for you to stay here with me, but I'm an old man, my child, I cannot look after a little girl. Now that Grandma has gone to be with God, I think it's best that I take you to your mother so she can look after you better than I could."

Grandpa and I sat at the train station and I leaned my head so it rested on his side. I was sad to be leaving the only place I ever knew and so I held on to Grandpa's hand. He looked down at me and winked as if to reassure me that everything would be all right. I didn't believe it would be and looking at my grandpa, I was sure he didn't believe it either.

"I'm scared, Grandpa."

He squeezed my hand but said nothing.

***

"Wake up. Wake up, you dirty goat."

I opened my eyes and saw my mother glaring down at me, she had a broom in her hand. The fog from my nightmare quickly faded away and the sad reality of my life made me jump up from my bed and retreat to the corner of the small room. My mother's cold expression made me feel even smaller than I was, and wretched. The only thing stopping me from bolting out the door was that I didn't have anywhere to go and right now, my mother wouldn't let me pass anyway.

She led me to the kitchen where she sat me down to tell me the rules.

"You will go to school until you finish your fourth grade and when you come home from school, I will have chores for you. I am not going to feed you for free so you will have to work hard."

It occurred to me that what she fed me I would not give to a pig and she knew that as well. I didn't understand the contempt she had for me or what I had done to deserve her cruelty. I started grade one at age seven and I finished grade two when Grandma died so I only had to finish another two years and then if she would let me, I would go on to secondary school.

Before long, I was walking to school in the morning and staying until three. My mother never gave me any food so the school allowed me to join the poor people and eat with them. When I came home from school the first time, my mother threw some clothes at me and pointed to the veranda, where she kept a stone washer with a scrubbing board. She gave me a bar of soap and told me to get to it. I went outside and tentatively put one of my stepfather's shirts in the water but the washer was higher than my height so I barely reached the scrub board.

"Get out of the way and I will show you how it's done," my mother spat, pushing me out of the way so I fell to the floor. She took the shirt and roughly scrubbed some soap on it, then washed it as if she was kneading bread, then she soaked it again and squeezed the water out of it by wringing it with her hands. When she finished, she pushed a small stool towards the washer, told me to stand on it and threw me another shirt.

"Now that you know how it's done, get to it, you—good for nothing."

I stood slightly higher than the washer now but I still struggled to pump my skinny arms to scrub the clothes clean. I dared not say anything or complain.

The third-floor apartment was small and old. Just inside the front door, the narrow hallway led left to the living room and right to the kitchen. In a corner of the kitchen was a table where we ate our meals and on the other side, a small counter where my mother prepared food, near the gas stove. Beside the counter was a faucet but no sink, just a low stone shelf with a bucket on it. At the end of the room and leading to an outside balcony, a stone toilet that didn't flush was built into the wall, a bucket of water sat beside it at all times.

***

It was the tenant's responsibility to keep the stairs leading to the apartments clean. The first time I had to scrub the stairs, I knelt on the third step from the top with a bucket of water, a bar of yellow soap, and a scrub brush so big I had trouble getting my hand around it. I heard my mother return from the market one day, then stop to talk with a neighbour on the first floor. I was about to call, *Ola Mae*—Hello Mom—when I heard the neighbour ask who I was.

My mother said, "Oh, that's my sister's daughter. You know, the one who lives in France."

I slipped back into the apartment, not making a sound. I didn't want her to know I had overheard. Her lying and shameful words crushed me.

I was told to address her boyfriend, Jaime, as *Padrinho*— godfather or stepfather—even though he never acknowledged my presence. At the end of every workday he whistled loudly while climbing the stairs, a signal for me to run and open the door for him. If I took too long and he had to wait, my mother hissed at me, berating me for being lazy. His arrival was the same every time. He greeted my mother by kissing her, then he picked up my baby sister, hugging and kissing her as well. He never even looked in my direction. It was as if a ghost had opened the door for him.

The first time my mother beat me was a few days after my grandfather left. She had bathed me the day before in the old steel bathtub she brought in from the veranda. I had never had a bath before, as we didn't have the facilities for it in my grandparents' house. Grandma had occasionally stripped me by the fire and washed me with a cloth while telling me stories. It was always done with a loving touch.

I don't remember if Grandpa had attempted to clean me or brush my hair before he took me to Lisbon, but my mother was quick to let me know I was filthy. In the bath, I was forced to stand naked and shivering in front of this woman who hated me. She made me feel dirty and ashamed, as if my unkempt appearance was my fault. I could tell by her scowl that she didn't even want to touch me but she had no choice. She rubbed my entire body with a cloth, then in an attempt to wash my hair, she scrubbed at my scalp with such force I suspect she was trying to wash the provincial life out of me.

My hair was long, curly and always dishevelled. She sat me at the kitchen table and cropped it short.

When I got up the next day and washed my face in the white plastic bowl she assigned to me, I could hear her cooing to the baby in her room. I had nothing with which to dry my face and still dripping, I searched the room not wanting to disturb her. When she'd bathed me the day before, she'd used a rag that at some time might've been a dress, but I couldn't see any sign of it anywhere. I knew she kept a clothesline in the hallway where she hung the washing if it rained, and I thought perhaps she had hung it there. I didn't see the dress so I snapped the clothespins off the smallest and oldest-looking towel and dried my face on it.

The cooing stopped. I heard my mother behind me and the tone of her voice made my legs weaken. "What are you doing?"

When I glanced up, her expression terrified me. What happened next was a blur and I never saw it coming. The palm of her hand slapped my face so hard that I reeled sideways and slammed into the wall, collapsing on the floor of the narrow corridor.

I didn't move or cry, just wrapped my arms around my head to protect myself from more strikes. She ripped the towel from my hand and informed me she didn't want some *poca de merda*—piece of shit—using her towels. She told me she would give me *um trapo*—a piece of cloth—which I was to use all the time.

"Don't let me catch you doing that again." she screamed. "These towels are not for the likes of you."

She stormed into the kitchen and threw the violated towel into the laundry basket.

A little dizzy, my face still hot and stinging from her slap, I slunk quietly into my room. I didn't give way to tears until I heard her go back to her room and my half-sister. Not wanting her to come after me again, I sat on my bed and wept silently. I had never felt so alone in my entire life. I didn't know what to do.

When I left the village with Grandpa, I took the only thing that belonged to my grandmother and I did not want to be without, a figure of Christ crucified. The old wood was now black and only the body of Jesus remained. The cross was gone and so were His arms but I adored it not only for what it represented, but because it had belonged to my grandmother. I kept it hidden from my mother but now, I took it out of the secret place.

With tears streaming down my face, I did what Grandma had always told me to do when I was sad. I brought my hands together and prayed to the only Father I knew, asking Him to help me cope with my new life. I knew I couldn't escape it but there had to be some way to at least improve it. I hoped desperately that God would hear my pleas. I needed to believe that He listened.

After I'd prayed for a while, I felt comforted and resigned. I headed to the kitchen to start working on whatever duties had been assigned to me that day. I had no other choice; I accepted that this was my destiny and I could only hope to endure it.

Except it had to be more than hope. I promised myself I would survive this miserable time in my life in spite of her. I didn't know how I would do it but ever since I'd put my hands together to pray, I'd known God was with me and I felt reassured. He was now the only positive thing in my life.

After that first time, every time my mother beat me, I went back to my room and knelt by my bed while the tears and the hurt washed over me.

The beatings continued. If I did a chore and my mother didn't approve, she slapped my face and told me I was a good-for-nothing "piece of shit". Sometimes her hand wasn't enough and she hit me with the broom, which she always kept handy.

"How many times do I have to teach you to do things right?" she screamed at me.

I learned that the best way to handle her outbursts was by keeping to myself. That way I had a slightly better chance of avoiding punishment.

Chapter Three

A Constant Craving

My stepfather rarely showed any emotion and my mother was submissive to his demands in every way. He always insisted on eating the best and freshest meals, so there was never a shortage of food in my mother's house. Not for them, anyway. If I was hungry, I waited until she wasn't in the living room where they kept the refrigerator, then grabbed something to eat. I only took what I thought she wouldn't miss, then I'd eat it while doing my chores.

One day, while ironing my stepfather's t-shirts, pants and underwear—a chore I hated doing—I didn't hear her come into the room.

"What are you eating?" she demanded.

"Nothing," I said, keeping my eyes on the ironing board.

"Don't lie to me," she growled. "I know you were in that fridge. Show me your hand."

She grabbed my arm and I closed my hand around the small piece of cheese I'd taken. She used her nails to pry my fingers open which made me drop the cheese. Seeing the evidence, she slapped me over and over again, screaming and hitting until I managed to get away and run to my room. She followed me but stopped on her way so she could pick up the broom from the kitchen. She cornered me where I cowered against the furthest corner of my bed, covering my head with my arms. I sobbed as my mother struck and I begged her to stop, but it kept on until she was too tired to continue.

The next day, a lock was installed on the refrigerator.

My mother went to the market early every morning, to buy whatever she was going to cook that day. She always came home with delicious-looking steaks and fish, cheese, sausage, and the most luscious apples, figs, and cherries, none of which I ever got to eat.

At mealtime, I sat at the table, my mouth watering as she set out the food. Leftovers were kept in the fridge for many days and she would grab the oldest one for me to eat.

Late one night, hungry and desolate, I knelt at the side of my bed holding on to the wooden Christ and pleaded with Grandma. "I miss you so much, Grandma. Please ask God to protect me from my mother. Please ask Him to look after me until I can look after myself."

***

For my half-sister's lunch, my mother mashed baby cookies and a banana in a bowl, then squeezed oranges and poured the juice over the mixture. If my mother happened to be in a particularly good mood, she would let me suck the remaining pulp from the orange skin.

When the baby finished eating, it was my job to pick her up and rock her until she fell asleep. My arms were thin and weak and Ana was not a small baby. To take my mind off the fatigue, I paced slowly from one end of the hall to the other, crooning softly, hoping my half-sister would fall asleep quickly. If it took her a long time, I feared my arms might fall off. When I finally laid her down, I hoped she was sound asleep because if she cried, my mother would come and push me out of the way, telling me I couldn't do anything right. Then she would lie on the bed with the baby, singing and gently patting Ana's soft little back until she fell asleep.

I remember when my mother brought home a rabbit for dinner. It had already been skinned and cleaned but she still had to cut it up. She did the work as she stood at the table, my half-sister playing on the floor at her feet. I stood beside my mother and looked longingly at the meat, imagining how tasty it would be once it was cooked. Noticing that, she picked up a kidney and gave it to me as if I were the family pet. I examined the smooth, clean piece of meat, then ate it. It didn't taste terrible and after that day, my mother always gave me the raw kidney as if it were a reward for good behaviour. If she was in a good mood, I got both kidneys.

When the rabbit had been cooked, I inhaled the delicious aromas that filled the kitchen, rising from the herbs and spices she mixed with it. But my mother was always able to find more leftovers in the fridge for me

Chapter Four

Into the Lion's Lair

I finished primary school at the age of eleven when my mother decided it was time that I found a job. I wanted to continue with my education but I had no choice. Once she got used to receiving money from me every week, I knew I would never make it back to school.

I found a job in a tailor's shop where I sewed buttons on jackets, swept the workroom floor and delivered suits to clients. After my first week, I took my pay home and my mother confiscated it with pleasure. She looked like she had won the lottery which, in a way she did, getting my money every week.

Every minute of my half-hour walks to work, I thought desperately about how to get away from her, or at least convince her to let me go back to school. If I didn't do something soon, I could be working at the tailor shop for the rest of my life. My mother never went to school and she ended up at my father's house. I did not want that fate for myself.

During the day, I had no time to do my house duties, so I swept and cleaned after work. So many times, as I scrubbed the kitchen floor after supper, I wished my mother would stop talking to the neighbours and do some of the work herself. She knew I'd been working all day. I wasn't able to scrub the living room after dark because the floor wouldn't dry and that would cause unnecessary humidity for the baby, so I had to do that room on Sundays.

It seemed so long ago that Grandma took me to church. I would've liked to go to church now but when I asked my mother, all she told me was that only zealots went to church. So, I secretly prayed for God to make my mother love me. I always felt comforted after that, as if I was sure God was going to grant me my request.

I became a woman that year, while working in the tailor's shop. All I had heard about "becoming a woman" were bits of gossip exchanged between my mother and her friends, but I didn't understand what was happening to my body. I had no idea how to deal with it. In a panic, I did what I could to stop the flow, then asked my mother about it when I got home. She backed away from me as if I had contracted an alien disease, then tossed me a couple of rags and instructed me on how to care for them. No tender motherly talk about the joys of being a young lady, no sweet words saying how proud she was to be my mother. All she had for me was disgust and contempt.

The dream of leaving my mother's house became an obsession. I couldn't stand the beatings any longer nor could I stand how depressed I was becoming. What did it matter, anyway, if I left? I would never be missed.

Not long after I started working at the tailors, my mother informed me that Dona Gabriela, a woman who lived on our street, said her sister needed an apprentice. Mrs. Santos made lampshades. She was looking for someone to deliver her work, pick up supplies and help at the shop. Since my mother had already volunteered my services to this woman, I had to quit my job with the tailor. I presumed either the pay was better, or my mother owed this woman some favours. The next day I took the streetcar to the address my mother gave me.

When Mrs. Santos answered the door and smiled at me, I knew immediately that I was going to enjoy working with her. She was pleasant and welcoming, showing me what her family business was all about. Two other women, Deolinda and Odete, worked there as well. Deolinda was the senior employee, and she was responsible for bringing the shades to the back room where Mrs. Santos' husband soldered them and did the final inspection before delivery.

For the first few days, I did small sewing jobs and after that, I shadowed Mrs. Santos wherever she went, learning the locations of all the suppliers and major clients. Although I still desperately wanted to go to school, I made the best of the situation, relieved to discover that I enjoyed my new job. It was different from sitting on a stool in a little room with a bunch of men, sewing buttons on jackets.

I thought Mrs. Santos was a wonderful woman. She was kind, accepting of me, and willing to teach me all I needed and wanted to know. She ran her business out of her home so I also helped her prepare meals and do her laundry when she was too busy. Sometimes, after the two women went home, or even on Saturdays, Mrs. Santos asked me to come in and help. I became her number one helper.

Mr. Santos was also kind and accepting, but what he wanted to teach me was something I didn't want to learn, something that made me curse him for the rest of his life and beyond.

Deolinda spent a lot of time bringing him shades to inspect. Sometimes I passed by his workroom and saw him pull his work apron down abruptly, as if to hide something. I thought that was odd at the beginning, but I was witnessing this more and more often. Deolinda seemed embarrassed but Mr. Santos would look at me and smile as he noticed me glancing into the room. One day, the same thing happened when I had to use the bathroom. I had to walk through his workroom and, as Deolinda walked away back to the sewing room, he put his apron down but lifted it again as I passed so I would see what he had in his hand. I didn't think what they were doing was right but it wasn't until then that I figured it out.

Once in the bathroom, I looked at my reflection in the mirror, my face red with embarrassment. I didn't want to come out of that bathroom for fear he would expose himself to me again. I had never seen a penis before and I was petrified that I was forced to look at it. When I finally came out, I didn't see him anywhere. When I returned to the sewing room, I passed by the front door and noticed his jacket was not hanging in its usual spot. He had gone out.

The next time Mrs. Santos left me alone in the house while she went to the beauty parlour, Mr. Santos was in the house as well. I wanted to stop her and beg her not to leave me alone but on the other hand, I didn't want to tell her what I saw, it was just too mortifying.

As I feared, shortly after his wife left, Mr. Santos came into the kitchen where I was preparing their dinner. Mrs. Santos had given me directions on what to do to prepare it.

"Lourdes, I know you saw what Deolinda and I were doing."

I didn't turn around hoping he would go away.

"It's nothing bad, you know, we just like playing. Would you like to play with me?"

I still didn't turn around but shook my head violently, keeping my gaze on what I was doing.

"Come here, Lourdes. Deolinda likes what we do and I know you are going to like it, too."

I shook my head again and prayed that this man would go away and leave me alone. I knew I didn't have a chance against this man. I was just a child and he was so tall and powerful.

Suddenly he was behind me, rubbing my back, and I didn't think it was his hand he used.

I could barely breathe. Mr. Santos knew my home situation. He knew they were paying me a decent wage and my mother would never take me away from them.

He grabbed my hand and brought it under his apron. I recoiled with disgust and shock.

He touched me with one hand and held me in place with the other.

"You are a beautiful girl, so pretty, so soft, let me touch you."

I crossed my legs and tensed up but he wouldn't stop.

"There is no harm in this and you'll like it, you'll see, let me see you," he said, his voice sickly sweet.

I shook my head vehemently but he took my hand and dragged me into his workroom. I pulled back, trying to get his hand off mine and begging him to leave me alone but his mind was made up as he pulled me behind him. I knew he was going to hurt me but I was powerless against this man.

He never pulled his pants entirely down, just in case his wife came home unexpectedly. Instead, he just undid the zipper and guided my head toward his erection. I stiffened with disgust as I felt his warm organ against my face. My mouth was tightly shut but he managed to part my lips and insert himself in my mouth. I gagged and began to heave when suddenly he let me go. He lifted me up and sat me on his worktable.

"Don't be afraid my little darling, this is very normal and if you let me do what I want, one day you will be a beautiful woman, as beautiful as a model, all because of what I will do to you. It will be our secret and you mustn't tell anyone—not your mother, your stepfather, or even my wife or Deolinda. They wouldn't believe you anyway and you like working here, don't you?"

I nodded because I thought that's what he wanted to hear and maybe he would let me go. He smiled then and touched me in my private parts. I squirmed and tried to get away from his strong grip but he was rough and powerful. He was insistent and determined and after a while when he wouldn't let me go, I gave up the fight. I shut down, pretending it wasn't happening.

He pressed my back against some rolls of silk, organza, velvet, and other materials they used in their craft, and I squeezed my eyes shut. In my mind I denied what was happening to me but I couldn't get away from his voice, droning on about how beautiful I would be when I grew up because of all the things he was going to teach me.

He kept repeating that this was our secret and I couldn't tell anyone because he would deny it and they would just call me a liar. With my eyes shut, I retreated to the deepest recesses of my mind, that way he couldn't touch the real me because I was no longer there.

But I do remember screaming.

The building they lived in was mostly populated by working

people and he knew no one would hear me.

Sometimes he gave me coins afterwards, along with a patronizing smile and repeated assurances that he was doing what was best for me.

I had secrets, not the kind of secrets eleven-year-olds have with a friend. My secret was with an old man. I had to learn to be resilient, to detach myself from those actions that were so foul, so nasty, and so damaging to my psyche. Actions that would be nightmares for the rest of my life. I felt sick to my stomach and cried every night when I went to bed, not only from my mother's beatings, but from this other helpless situation. I couldn't tell anyone. My mother would probably kill me if I did, so I accepted my fate. I had nowhere to go and no one in this world gave a damn about me.

When I turned fourteen, in spite of the shame I felt in Mr. Santos' house, I dreaded going home after work even more. I never knew what awaited me there. Some days my mother was relaxed and left me alone with my chores. She had never been friendly towards me, but she did have days when she could at least be merely "indifferent". At other times she was waiting for me, prepared to make my life even more miserable.

If I arrived home and saw she was having a bad day, I tried to stay in my bedroom until I was summoned. If her mood seemed to be that of indifference, I still tread carefully, but slightly less so.

One night, I misread her mood and wasn't able to detect it until it was too late. I slouched through the door, feeling exhausted, tired of walking all day weighed down by shopping bags and lampshades. My mother stood in the kitchen preparing dinner and since I didn't sense any particular threat, I relaxed and sat at the table, the only place to sit. I wished I could talk with her about my day, about what was going on in my life that left me so without hope, but I knew she wouldn't be interested.

No one else was in the kitchen and I felt relatively safe sitting there. My stepfather and my half-sister were in the living-room. My mother stood by the stove, arranging an octopus on an overturned bowl set on a platter. The octopus's tentacles had been carefully draped over the bowl, so they would be easy to cut from all sides of the table. That was dinner. After studying its slimy corpse, it was with relief that I wondered what leftovers I would be given, thinking anything was better than octopus. She set the creature in the middle of the table and glared at me.

"All you want is rest, isn't it?" she asked, suddenly not indifferent at all.

I had misjudged her mood.

"All you want is to sit there like a queen and be served." She bowed in mockery, extending her hand towards the table.

Not knowing what else to do and hoping to avoid any additional fury, I turned my head away. That was a mistake because I immediately felt a hard, stinging blow to the back of my head. She'd hit me with such force I actually thought my neck had snapped.

Her voice was ice cold. "Don't turn your head on me, you lazy bitch." She spat out her words.

As she lifted her hand to hit me again, I jumped to my feet and ran to my room, hoping she wouldn't come after me, feeling very relieved when she didn't. I slid closed the curtain that served as a door, not wanting my stepfather or half-sister to see my pain when they went into the kitchen for dinner.

Since it was such a tiny apartment, the living room wasn't far from the kitchen. My stepfather overheard everything. From behind the curtain, I couldn't see him passing my room but I heard his chair being pulled back from the table. That's how I knew he had sat down. After a moment he told Ana, "Go call the kid to come and eat."

"No, you don't." my mother shouted. "You sit down and eat your food." I heard Ana squeak as our mother pushed her towards her chair. Ana missed the chair and ended up on the floor, crying. Furious, my stepfather stood up and slapped my mother's face.

My entire body shook with fear behind the curtain. This fight was my fault and I would suffer the consequences later. Across from my curtain, the hallway curved to the right and led into the kitchen. I stepped out and stood in the hallway, listening and trying to make sense of what was going on. I didn't have to see my mother to know how angry she was, by the sound of her voice.

"She just came home and sat like a princess, expecting me to serve her." she yelled. "She can go without food."

"The kid did nothing, Angelina," my stepfather said.

I couldn't believe my ears. He'd never defended me before, or looked at me, for that matter. While I was grateful that he'd stood up for me, I wasn't sure if he'd just made things worse.

"I heard everything," he continued. "Sometimes she deserves to be punished and you do nothing. Clearly, today she was just sitting there."

My mother's fury punctuated every word. "What do you care what I do to her? She's no concern of yours. Why? Why all of a sudden do you care what I do with her?"

"I don't care," he said, his voice calm. "If she deserves to be punished, then I don't care, but the kid did nothing this time. You're behaving like a crazy woman."

I inched my way closer and peeked from around the darkened corridor. What I saw frightened me beyond belief. My mother stood in the middle of the kitchen, bashing her own head with clenched fists. My stepfather had sat again and was trying to console my half-sister who was frightened and crying louder than ever. When my mother stopped hitting herself, her eyes sparkled with a crazed look.

She pointed a trembling finger at her boyfriend. "If I find out there is something going on between you and her, I'll kill her."

He got up again and faced her, his cool expression replaced by a stony anger. He spoke quietly but firmly. "You are a stupid woman, Angelina, and I think you must've lost your senses."

He picked up my half-sister and headed for the living room while I rushed back behind the curtain. My mother had just accused me of such a vile act I almost wished for death. I wanted to disappear, run from the house, from my mother's life, from my life, from this world. I didn't think my defeated, defiled and humiliated spirit could take much more.

My stepfather never even looked at me. If, in the past, he'd ever wanted to communicate anything to me, he did it either through my mother or my half-sister. Defending me this time had been the kindest thing he had ever done, and my mother had to make it look dirty and shameful. Through what she'd said, she was insinuating that I had been abused by him and if that were so, then it would be my fault. All I could think of was Mr. Santos and his breathy assurances that I had to keep his abuse to myself. It was my dirty secret, my problem. As I thought about all this, anger surged through me as the tears rushed out and my brain threatened to burst out of my head. My mother's words not only reflected her cruelty, they deepened my shame.

A little later, my stepfather left, as usual, to go to the pub. I felt completely alone but determination burned in me. This woman, this monster who was my mother could not get away with stomping my soul like a bug underfoot. I would not perish into total desperation. I had no one to watch over me, I had to face the monster.

I slid the curtain aside and walked into the kitchen. She paced back and forth, muttering words I couldn't make out and I wanted to run back into my little room. I was intimidated but I was so angry with her. She would probably end up killing me but I had to defend myself, I had to tell this woman what I thought of her insinuations. My pain and indignity of the situation had taken over and I knew I had to defend my honour.

As soon as she saw me, she picked up the broom, but even that didn't stop me.

"Do you know what you just insinuated about me? How can you say such vile things about your own daughter?" The dam burst and I didn't bother holding back the tears. "Do you realize I'm just a kid? An orphan? An abandoned child?"

"Shut up or you'll get the broom, you cow!" she shouted.

"So, hit me." I shouted, raising my arms. "Go ahead, kill me. That would be better than humiliating me the way you just did." I narrowed my eyes and glared at her, lowering my voice with such intention that she was forced to listen. "Who are you? You can't possibly be my mother," I hissed. "You should be ashamed of yourself. One day…one day I hope you will need me the way I've needed you. That will be a great day for me. That's the day when I will remind you of everything you've done to me."

I turned and headed back to my bedroom, still crying but noticing how light my heart felt now that I had spoken up. Still, nothing I'd said could change what had happened or what would continue to happen. I could never again face my stepfather but despite my bravado, I knew my mother still hated me.

She followed me to my room. Sitting on my bed, I looked up expecting her to hit me with the broom, hoping in a way that she would put me out of my misery, I didn't care anymore. But she simply pointed at me and her words were thick with revulsion and venom.

"Me?" she said, pointing at herself. Then she pointed at me. "Need a piece of shit like you? Don't worry, I'm never going to need YOU."

She threw the broom at my feet and turned away, storming towards the living room. I didn't see her for the rest of the evening. When there were no more tears to shed, I went into the kitchen and cleaned up the supper dishes, despite the fact I hadn't eaten a thing.

I didn't consider her my mother any more. She was nothing more than a hateful person I had to accept as part of my life. Yes, she had taken me in when I'd had no place else to go, but she was so cruel, God, she was cruel. Every night I held Grandma's broken crucifix and prayed for the strength to go on for one more day.

I was so tired of it all.

Chapter Five

Afonso's Child

I tried to find ways to a better life and never stopped weighing the possibilities of this and that. My mother wasn't always a monster, although her "friendly" moments with me were few and far between. After the kitchen episode was forgotten and everyone was talking to each other again, I decided to approach my mother about my father. One day while my stepfather was at work, I left my humble bedroom where I always felt safe, (unless my mother was on the warpath, then there was no safe place anywhere) and ventured into the living room where she was playing with my half-sister. I looked into the room and sensing my presence, she looked directly at me, disinterested, but quickly went back to tickling Paulo, my new baby brother. Ana giggled and clapped her hands, hoping to get some attention as well.

"Mother, can I ask you something?"

"What do you want?" was her quick reply.

"I don't know anything about my father. Would you mind telling me about him and his family?"

"Your father was a piece of shit like you," she snapped.

"Why do you say that? Was he a really bad man?"

"He ruined my life, so yes, he was a bad man." She went back to playing with the baby. I wasn't sure if I should continue or just go away. I decided to persevere although I knew to use caution.

"What was his name?"

"Afonso," she continued still not looking at me.

"Did you love him?"

"Love him? Of course I didn't love him; he was my boss."

She scowled and I kept silent, hoping she'd continue. Her face looked angry now and I was getting worried.

She turned her gaze to the baby who was on a blanket on the floor and her face softened as she looked at him. I waited patiently. She picked the baby up and settled him on her lap while Ana moved closer to her and sat quietly, probably wondering what the conversation was all about.

My mother shrugged as her gaze settled on me and the look on her face was as if she had gone back in time. Pensive and quiet.

"I looked after them and their children," she said. "I cooked their meals, made their beds and picked up all their shit, and for that he figured he could have his way with me. I couldn't escape, he was determined."

"Where was his wife?" I ventured.

"His wife was a spoiled woman who never lifted a finger to help with anything. She rarely even acknowledged my presence except to tell me what my duties were around her house."

I felt the growing anger, the helplessness and the disappointment in her voice, but I couldn't stop now. "Did my father know about me?"

"Oh yes, my sister came to Granja just after you were born and it didn't take her long to pick you up and take you to Joao Durao. She wanted your father to meet you."

She placed the baby back on the blanket and got up, walking to the window and looking out into the distance. She laughed bitterly.

"What happened?" I asked, curious and hoping she would answer my endless questions.

"What happened?" she asked turning back to me. "Your aunt walked through the whole village with you in her arms and didn't hesitate to stop everyone and tell them you were Afonso's child. She finally reached your father's house and still holding you, knocked at their door."

I couldn't let her stop, no matter what.

"Did they open the door for her?"

"Your siblings opened the door and by now a small crowd had followed your aunt but, in the house, someone came behind the children and slammed the door on your aunt's face."

" What happened then?" I asked, this was great.

"Your aunt stepped away from the door and looked up at the windows, lifting you in the air and yelling, "This is your daughter, Afonso. Take a good look, you coward'."

"He never came out to see me?" I asked, heartbroken.

"Why would he? Him and his wife taught the village's children, they no longer had a future there. Your aunt destroyed them." A triumphant smile played at the corners of my mother's mouth.

"Is that when they went to Brazil?"

"It is. Now go away."

She went back to playing with her children. I was stunned by all that I learned from my mother. I didn't think I would ever get to meet my father, nor would I ever get rescued by him. It dawned on me that I was probably just a bad memory, as far as he was concerned. I did learn something though, was I not in a similar situation as my mother? Except that I wasn't pregnant, not as far as I knew. I loved to read so I read a lot of books and I knew I could get pregnant but then what? What would I do? I thought about that all the time and I couldn't imagine anything more terrifying. Would Mr. Santos run to Brazil like my father did? I wish he would do it now.

This was too much for me to absorb, it gave me headaches and nightmares. I didn't want to become a sad and angry person like my mother. Was that why she was so mean to me? Because I reminded her of my father? Was that my fault?

A few days after this conversation with my mother, I became ill. My throat hurt so much I could hardly swallow. Through my pain I begged my mother to take me to a doctor and, reluctantly, she did.

The doctor said I had tonsillitis and he told my mother he would have to take my tonsils out, soon.

A few days later, I sat with my mother and siblings in the doctor's waiting room, my head swimming with terrifying thoughts of what was about to happen. Would this hurt more than the pain I already felt? Would there be lots of blood? What if the doctor makes a mistake and kills me?

The nurse called my name and led me to a room where the doctor stood waiting. My mother followed with my siblings and was told to sit in the corner. I was taken to a chair with an overhanging light attached and a shining tray of operating utensils lying to one side of it. The doctor smiled reassuringly but that did nothing to calm my nerves. My mother held Paulo on her knee and Ana stood beside her. I glanced towards my mother for some hint of encouragement but all I got was an expressionless stare. I looked up at the doctor and noticed the compassion in his eyes as he tilted my head backward to look into my throat.

As nice as that was, it wasn't his compassion I needed at that moment. I needed my mother's, I was terrified. If only she could have given me one small smile of encouragement to help me feel brave. Instead, she sat rigidly while the doctor inserted a long needle into my mouth. Although my head was firmly held in place by the nurse, if I looked out the corner of my eye, I could still see my mother. I kept my eyes on her and couldn't help it when tears overflowed. The doctor looked at me with alarm and asked if he was hurting me but I managed to shake my head, assuring him there was no pain. I could feel him pulling at my throat, but that was all.

It wasn't the doctor's scalpel cutting my flesh that made me cry, it was the agony of my mother's disdain tearing up my soul. Her cruel dismissal touched almost every moment of my life in her house.

When the whole ordeal was over, I walked home beside my mother, in silence, because she never had anything to say to me. The doctor had told her to buy me an ice cream on the way and she did that, but there was no joy when she handed it to me. I slurped it up because the coolness of it felt good in my throat, but tears falling from my eyes prevented me from enjoying such a wonderful treat.

When I'd lived in Granja with my grandparents, I never got presents for Christmas because we couldn't afford them. Instead, my grandmother made the day special by taking me to church and telling me the story of the baby Jesus. I loved listening to her and admired the strength of her faith.

In my mother's home we never went to church because she didn't believe in God. I never got any Christmas presents there either, but my half-sister and half-brother always did. One Christmas morning when Paulo was still a toddler, my stepfather led him and Ana into the kitchen. I saw them passing my room on the other side of the curtain and I cautiously stepped out to see what was going on.

My stepfather guided them to where he had hung two socks just above the stove, but told the children that *Pai Natal* (Santa Claus) had left them there. He smiled at Ana and Paulo tenderly, as if they were his whole world, and my heart twisted with envy. While I sat at the table and watched, he pulled a gold necklace out of the socks for each of them. My mother stood by. They looked the ideal family then and I knew that I didn't belong there. Nobody acknowledged my presence. My half-sister jumped up with joy and my half-brother babbled excitedly as he shared my half-sister's enthusiasm.

Secretly, I hoped there would be something for me, anything to tell me they cared, but there were only two socks hanging above the stove.

That never changed.

Chapter Six

Grandpa

The years passed and my life continued the same, both at my
mother's home and at my job. Sometimes my mother would still take
out her frustrations on me and sometimes she could be tolerable. I
never stopped hoping for a better future. Almost sixteen, I had lived
with my mother for seven years and in that time, I learned a lot. I
learned to self-preserve, to avoid confrontations with my mother and
to try and stay away from Mr. Santos. The latter was difficult
because if he wanted to use me, he'd just announce the workday
over and send the women home. He would then convince his wife to
take a trip to the beauty salon, to relax. By not despairing and
submitting to my destiny, perhaps I could survive this time in my life
with as little harm as possible to my psyche.

The day after I turned sixteen, we received a letter from cousin

Filomena in Granja. I read it aloud to my mother, trying to still the tremble in my voice as I read that Grandpa was very sick. Filomena asked for someone to come at once but my mother wanted nothing to do with my grandfather or the village. I begged her to let me go instead and surprisingly, she agreed. And because of the urgency in Filomena's letter, we decided I should leave for Granja early the next day. At the train station as she bought my ticket, my mother shocked me when she gave me a little extra money for a taxi.

"To get to and from Granja to the train station," was all she said.

All the familiar heartache rushed back in when I remembered how Grandma had died without medical assistance. I feared for Grandpa. The women in the village had occasionally taken care of Grandma but I doubted Grandpa had been so lucky. He depended on Filomena's compassion but she had a family that kept her busy and I was positive she didn't see Grandpa on a daily basis. Poverty makes a difference, especially whether a person receives proper health care. Grandpa was poor, he had nothing.

On the train and in spite of my sadness, it was good to get out of Lisbon even if it was just temporary. As I looked out the window, the city buildings were left behind and after a couple of hours I noticed more fields, rocky fields I didn't remember seeing on my way to Lisbon. And then pasture fields started to appear and it looked a lot more like the landscape I use to see in my infancy. A memory came forth.

When I started grade one, the Gamboas', the healthiest family in the village, had asked Grandpa if I would take their cows to pasture on weekends. I didn't mind that, the cows grazed all day and it gave me the chance to read all the books Miss Alcina lent me. Sometimes I would lay on my back on the grass and I would daydream of being like the children in my storybooks.

When the sun began its descent, I would put my books away and find a stick so I could guide the cows to get going by tapping them on the rump. One day, I began to gather the cows but some of them were just happy lying on the ground or munching on the grass. By the time I got them heading in the direction of home, the sun lay low on the horizon. Darkness was fast approaching and I couldn't make the cows go any faster. When the sun set, both sides of the dirt road looked dark and scary and I knew I was still quite a way from home. In my active imagination, I envisioned wolves coming out of the woods and walking slowly and menacing towards me, teeth bared and eyes glowing. In my story books, I had read a story about a similar situation and I couldn't wait to get to Grandma's house. I had a brief thought of trying to mount one of the cows so I would be up high, but I knew I would never be able to manage that, they were just so big. After a while I could hardly see where I was going, I just followed the cows and hoped they knew their way home. More ominous thoughts entered my mind. What if I stepped on a venomous snake and got bit by it? I would die on that lonely road. I decided to be brave and think of happy thoughts.

Maybe next weekend I would ask my cousin Tony who was twelve and afraid of nothing, to come and help me take the cows home.

Thinking about these scary but happy days in the village with Grandma and Grandpa made me smile. The train was going fast but I could still see small houses in the distance, and animals in the fields. I still had a few hours to get to Grandpa, so I let myself remember.

The next weekend Tony went with me and stayed all day. We climbed the fig trees and had lunch sitting up high on the large branches and reaching for the fruit with satisfaction. After lunch we sat in the shade on the tree while the cows grazed. Most of the time we would talk. Tony was the oldest of five children and he knew his mother's husband was not his father.

"Ever think about your father?" he asked.

"I do, all the time." I said sadly.

"Do you want me to go with you to Joao Durao? We could find out where he lives now and maybe you could write to him"

For an instant, his words ignited a spark of hope in me and I thought how wonderful it would be to meet my father. Then reality set in.

"I don't think so, he doesn't care about me. I bet he doesn't know who I am or that I exist." I said, breaking the little stick I was playing with into many small pieces. "What about you, Tony, do you ever think about your real Dad?" I asked, looking up at him.

"I do once in a while but I don't bother with it for very long."

"Why? Wouldn't you want to know who he is?"

"Look here," he said, "Yours doesn't care about you, what makes you think mine would care about me?" Tony didn't look at me as he spoke but I knew the pain in his heart was as big as mine.

"Let's get going, time to take the cows home."

When we arrived to the Gamboas' and got the cows into the barn, one of the women called to us to come into the house. We had never been inside and we sat in the living room and admired its sumptuousness. The big room was warmed by a big brazier in the centre of it, filled with live coals.

When the woman finally came back, she held in her hands exotic-looking round and oval candies in lovely shades of soft pinks, greens and blues. I held mine in my hand admiring them. I didn't dare to eat them; they were so pretty. They were like small objects of art, tiny in size but decorated with well-defined flowers and leaves.

On the way home, I held the candy gently in my hand.

"You shouldn't eat those" Tony said pointing at them.

"I'm not going to, right away, but why shouldn't I eat them?" I asked curious.

"They are poisonous, they will make you sick. Look how weird they look, have you ever seen candy like that?"

"I don't believe you." I defended. "Why would they give us poisoned candy that would make us sick?"

"They don't care about you, to them you're just the kid who guards the cows. I bet if you eat the candy and die, they'll probably ask me to do your job. Here, give them to me, I will get rid of them for you."

I believed him. I was about to place the precious candies in his hands when suddenly he keeled over, laughing hysterically. "You believed me," he laughed, pointing at me. I slapped his hand and turned towards home but I too was overcome with laughter.

"You would've given me the candy, wouldn't you?" he asked as we resumed our walk.

"I would not." I said, hiding a smile.

"You would so, but don't worry, I would save a couple for you." He said, putting his arm around my little shoulders as we walked side by side, savouring some of the candy together.

I came out of my reverie when the train arrived in Vila Franca das Naves. The sun shone a brilliant and hot sphere in a cloudless sky. I disembarked and looked around, seeking a taxi. The adventure of travelling on my own made me feel independent and free as I stood outside the station with my old suitcase. My worry over

Grandpa's wellbeing mingled with the anticipation of returning to my childhood home, held me almost breathless.

When a taxi finally pulled up and drove us along the unpaved roads, everything we passed, especially the mimosa trees, aroused melancholy in me. I clearly recalled travelling these dusty roads with Grandpa and begging him to lower the branches of the mimosa trees so I could collect a bouquet of fluffy yellow blooms for Grandma. A knot of emotion rose up in my throat and I said a prayer for Grandpa as we approached the village.

When the car stopped in front of Grandpa's dwelling, I was astonished by what I saw. As a child, I would climb the outside wall that surrounded our stone house and plant a garden of soil and wild flowers on top, wanting to make our house look pretty from the street. Now, that same wall stood no taller than my knees. It wasn't even a wall anymore, just a broken-down pile of stones. The tiny yard I played in so long ago was much smaller, only a couple of steps from the pile of stones to the door.

I got close and put my ear to the door, hoping to hear sounds from inside. I knocked a couple of times and no one answered so I thought perhaps Grandpa wasn't home. The old door held a look of decay. The loose upper hinge kept the door at a forty-five-degree angle, half in and half out of the opening.

"Grandpa, are you here?" I called.

Silence.

I squeezed through the opening and stepped inside. Daylight streamed in behind me and illuminated the small room, leaving me dumbfounded.

It had been so long since I had last seen my childhood home. I hardly remembered what it once looked like but now everything looked tiny, dirty, and rundown. On my left, what used to be a kitchen stood empty. The armoire I remembered was gone, likely burned for warmth long ago. I could still see what looked like ashes in the hearth where Grandma cooked all our meals. There hadn't been a fire there in a very long time.

In the wall ten feet ahead of me, a small window allowed a sliver of light into the space, its glass broken for so long that green moss clung to its jagged edges. The place smelled of mildew and dirt. Grandpa's house was cold, dark, damp, and clearly unsuitable for a human being to live in.

I heard a soft moan and turned to find its source on my right, but I wasn't ready for what I found.

What was left of Grandpa lay on rags on the dirt floor of the tiny little space where I used to sleep, covered with a worn and dirty blanket. His crevassed face was emaciated and old, and although his eyes were open, I suspected little life remained within. Overcome with sorrow, I knelt beside him and took his limp hand in mine.

"Grandpa," I whispered. "Can you hear me? It's me, Grandpa, I'm here."

He struggled to turn his head towards me and when he realized who I was, tears filled his eyes and streamed down the sides of his face. Seeing he could not speak without a great deal of effort, I leaned closer so I could hear the last words he would ever say to me, "My little one, my darling little Lourdes, I'm so glad you're here."

He had been left with no one to care for him, no one to love him. He had cousins in the village and they probably brought him food, but that had been the extent of their care. So alone, so afraid and so very ill—had he suffered a stroke? He could barely manage to clutch my hands with his, hanging on as though he never wanted to let go.

I looked around the house for food and water but saw none. Nor was there anything in which to store food or cook it, even the three-legged iron pot was gone.

"I'm going to get you some food, Grandpa," I told him, squeezing his hand with reassurance. "I'll be right back."

Cousin Filomena's house was on the other side of the village. I sobbed as I ran, not caring who saw me. When I arrived, I asked my cousin what had happened to Grandpa and all she told me was that he had taken to his bed some time before and he hadn't been seen outside since.

Filomena and I returned to Grandpa's house with some broth and I tried to spoon some of the liquid through his parted lips. A gurgling sound told me he wasn't swallowing; I had come too late. Grandpa was dying and there wasn't a damn thing I could do about it.

I held his hand, closed my eyes and thanked God for allowing me to be of some comfort to Grandpa at the end of his life, just as he had been for me at the beginning of mine. I was glad to be there.

I sat and talked to him not expecting a response, only hoping the sound of my voice might soothe him. I talked about when I was a child, remembering happy stories about when I lived with him and Grandma, good times we'd had in spite of hardship and poverty.

"I loved it when you played your flute for us, Grandpa. Out in the fields when you guarded the sheep and Grandma and I brought you your dinner. The sounds you made had Grandma and me smiling and swaying to the sounds of your music. I love you Grandpa."

It was dark outside when Filomena came back and insisted that I get some rest. I didn't want to leave Grandpa, but I ended up doing as she asked. I was exhausted and she was right, there was nothing to sit or lie down on, only the cold floor. Grandpa seemed peaceful so I adjusted his blanket, told him I would be back soon and then left with my cousin.

In the morning, I returned and opened the door to a horrific sight that will stay with me as long as I live. I will never know what Grandpa's feverish mind had forced him to do but I will never forget its effects. Somehow, he had crawled out of his bed, dragged his naked body across the floor and now lay on the entrance floor, dead. He had been tormented over his final hours, plainly terrified of something. Scratches covered his body, bearing witness to his desperate efforts to flee whatever he thought was chasing him.

I covered his naked shell and knelt on the old floor, cradling his head in my lap. He had died recently, his hand still warm in mine. In my anguish, clutching my grandfather and rocking him against me, I felt certain he had been waiting for me to return to Granja so he could go. Between sobs I cried, "I'm sorry Grandpa. I'm so sorry I wasn't here with you."

I asked God to embrace my grandpa and give him peace in His kingdom, to make up for all the suffering on this earth.

He was buried for free on one side of the cemetery reserved for those who cannot afford to pay. The only people who attended the funeral were Filomena's family and myself. After the burial, I looked for Grandma's grave but was told it wasn't hers anymore. In such a small cemetery, when a grave hasn't been paid for it is recycled after seven years. My grandma's grave was now the resting place for some other poor soul. I knew where it had been, though, so I stopped and said a little prayer for Grandma. I thanked her again for being the only mother I ever knew.

After Grandpa's funeral, all I wanted was to leave the sad village of Granja. There was nothing else there I cared about. I would've gladly stayed and lived the simple life, if only the two people I had loved so much were still there. How good it would've been to forget about city life with all its corruptions. I would leave my mother's house in an instant and forget I ever had a mother, if only my grandma and grandpa were still with me.

When I returned to Lisbon and told my mother the sad events, I expected her to mourn Grandpa's death with me but all I got was silence and indifference.

Chapter Seven

A Real Education

In 1969, Portugal was still under the influence of Antonio Salazar, who had died the previous year. Salazar was one of the least-known European dictators and controlled the country for almost forty years. His influence was so strong that little changed after he died. Salazar's policies led to the country's economic and social stagnation as well as rampant immigration. His authoritarian government had turned the country into one of the poorest in all of Europe.

As a result, Portugal suffered from one of the highest rates of illiteracy in the world. People like me were discouraged from seeking an education because the fees for registration into secondary schools were impossibly high. If you were poor, a basic education covering grades one to four was taught with great rigour and was granted to all citizens.

By the end of grade four, I knew how to read and write well. I had some knowledge of geography, math, history, religion, and calligraphy. Now at sixteen years old, I desperately wanted to go back to school. Otherwise, I would never escape my miserable life. Out of curiosity, I went to one of the secondary schools and asked about evening education, knowing full time studies were out of the question. I was told classes would be starting in September, just four months away.

I knew my mother would try to prevent me from going and I didn't have much time in which to convince her. I remember one day, a long time ago when I came home with one of the books my teacher had lent me, and I didn't understand a sentence.

I heard Grandma's voice in my head.

"*Agua mole em pedra dura, tanto da ate que fura...*Persistence, my child. If you have a goal or you wish for anything hard enough, you can attain it through hard work, faith, and persistence. Never forget that."

I never forgot that advice from such a loving and dear soul as my grandma. Now I would put that advice into action to free myself not only from my mother, but from the man who kept me as a sex slave.

One night, just before I fell asleep, a plan formed in my mind. As a delivery girl, I was often given tips which I used to buy books. I loved to read, to immerse myself in a good story and pretend I was in another world, another life, where I was the heroine. Now I would put that money to better use.

By morning, I envisioned a plan to start building a future, block by tiny block.

On my way downtown the next morning, I took a detour and ended up at Josefa D'Obidos, one of Lisbon's secondary schools. When I asked about their evening studies program, I was told I would need seventy-five escudos to register. That, to me, seemed like a small fortune but I had to try. In the end, it took me almost a month to save that much.

"I would like to go back to school," I told my mother, matter of fact, one evening.

She sat at the table, spooning food into Paulo's mouth. I was washing the dinner dishes and from the corner of my eye, I saw her turn her head in my direction but she said nothing.

"I would like to study and maybe get a better job someday," I said, washing up another plate.

"There's nothing wrong with your job."

I shrugged. "Maybe not, but I don't want to be an apprentice to Mrs. Santos all my life."

"And why not?" Her voice was sharpening. I had to be careful. "What other job do you think you can do?"

"I don't know, but if I get a secondary school diploma, there would be options."

"What options? What are you talking about?" She pushed the spoon at Paulo, dismissing me. "Just do the dishes and leave me alone. I don't want to hear about any school."

"But I want to learn more, I know I can do it but I have to go to school."

"I never went to school," she said, looking back at me. "You don't need to, either. Besides, you already have a job."

I couldn't help raising my voice a little louder than I should have. "Are you punishing me just because you never went to school?"

"I will punish you if you don't shut up," she shouted, irritated.

"But, Mother, don't you see?" I asked gently. "I could make more money for you if I had a better job but to do that, I need to go to school."

"And how would Your Excellency pay for it?" she asked sarcastically.

I hated when she called me "Your Excellency", but it wasn't as bad as some of the other names she called me.

"I'll find a way somehow," I said.

"No, the answer is no." she declared, eyes wide with determination.

I wasn't getting anywhere with her at that point so I stopped talking. I would have to think of a way to change her mind, gently.

Over time, I learned to manipulate my mother. If I bought her a present, she acted kindly towards me and that way I avoided her anger. It didn't have to be an expensive present, perhaps just a pair of stockings, an embroidered handkerchief, or a bottle of wine. I soon learned the meaning of the word "bribery" and it became an excellent tool in my arsenal.

One day my mother asked me how I got the money to buy the gifts for her. I told her people sometimes gave me tips. Of course, she demanded all my wages but she had no idea what tips I got or when. I hid every penny, then I took out small amounts to spend on her throughout the summer. Things seemed to be improving between us. She seemed a little happier. She still got upset with me at times, but I hadn't been beaten in a while. Occasionally, she even invited me to go out with her, Ana, and Paulo, even if it was just heading to the park in front of the train station. During these rare times I almost felt as if I were part of the family, such was my fervent wish to be so, not a total outsider.

We were getting along well enough that I almost felt bad when I had to bribe her, but I had no other choice. It was time.

I took advantage of her good mood one day and brought up the subject of going to school. To my astonishment, she didn't get angry. She simply told me that if I really wished to go to school, I could.

I was well aware she might change her mind any day as she often did, so I made sure I was on my best behaviour from then on and continued to make her happy with little favours.

When registration day arrived, I could hardly wait to get off work. I took two different streetcars to get to Josefa D'Obidos and register for my first year of secondary school. The more I thought about it the more excited I became. As I pushed through the school's front door, I became aware of my sweaty palms. I paused a moment, looking around and thinking how wonderful it would be to belong here. I saw a woman sitting behind a large desk so I approached.

"Excuse me, is this where I register for evening classes?"

"Yes, it is, here, fill this out," the woman said, handing me a form.

I looked for a chair and began filling this form. When I finished, I dug in my purse for the money that took me so long to save and headed back to the desk. I presented the woman with the form and the money but she glanced up at me with a pained expression. "I'm sorry my dear but you don't have enough money, the fee to register is eighty escudos."

I stared at her a moment, speechless. What was I going to do? Seventy-five escudos was all the money I had and it had been so hard to accumulate that much. I had enquired at the school some time earlier that year and had been told it would be seventy-five escudos.

"May I use your phone, please."

"Yes, you may, there's one on the wall, there." She pointed behind me.

Head lowered and feeling very disappointed, I headed towards the phone and tentatively picked up the receiver.

I considered the registration situation to be of the utmost importance, so I called Dona Helena, our neighbour who had a phone. When my mother finally came on the line, she sounded out of breath and when I told her why I had called, she was furious.

"The answer is no." she shouted.

"But you said I could go to school and I only need five escudos."

"I don't care what I said, I changed my mind." She hung up.

Tears welled up in my eyes and I stood holding the phone, trying to hide my distress. I was already embarrassed for not having enough money, I couldn't go back to the desk now and tell the woman my mother thought I didn't need to go to school.

I couldn't spend the rest of my life living with my mother, being beaten and abused. I'd end up like her, or worse.

I wanted an education; I needed an education. I absolutely refused to give up that easily.

My next best option was to call Mrs. Santos. I couldn't help crying as I told her why I had called, apologizing all the while. She told me to calm down because when I came to work the following day, she would give me the money I needed. Then I could return to the school and finish registering.

When I got home that evening, the dirty supper dishes were waiting for me and my meal of old leftovers found their way to the table as well. My whole body sagged as I looked at everything, feeling unhappy and discouraged. I forced dinner down, washed the dishes and went to bed. My mother hadn't said anything to me about my phone call and I didn't tell her I had called Mrs. Santos.

The next day, a smiling Mrs. Santos gave me the money I needed and I thanked her for her kindness.

"Don't worry about it, it's a gift from me to you."

Money in hand, I returned to the school at the end of the day and paid for my registration. With every breath I became more resolved to study hard, get a good job, make a life for myself no matter what. I was determined to take charge of my destiny.

September came, bringing with it my first day of school. It seemed I was the only new student because everyone else laughed and talked with each other. It felt peculiar, sitting in a classroom with so many people who obviously knew more than I did. It had been years since I had been in a school and I hoped I wasn't too stupid to continue. Years before, Miss Alcina had told Grandpa that I was smart, so I tried my best not to disappoint my grandparents or Miss Alcina, even though they weren't there to see it.

I was new to everything. I watched students raise their hands to ask questions but I was too shy to raise mine. Besides, I had no clue what to ask anyway. Even if I had been brave enough to ask something, would the answer be so obvious they would all laugh at me? Sometimes when I heard the answer, I realized I'd known it already, but I still couldn't get myself to ask anything. So, I listened hard and did the assignments.

At the end of the school year, I passed with good grades. I told my mother I was doing well in school but she didn't seem to care.

Every time I opened my notebook, I got excited. I loved learning new things. To me, school was a great adventure. It made the difference between a good future and becoming a replica of my mother. That awful thought gave me the courage to strive towards my goal.

The physical part of going to school depended upon how my mother felt at the end of each day. Many times, I rushed out in tears because she'd delayed me, giving me extra chores to do or telling me I wouldn't be going to school that evening. I couldn't make her understand that I shouldn't miss class. One day, after giving her another small gift, I tried to persuade her that it would be much easier for me to go to school if I left directly from work. She never gave me an answer so I presumed that would be fine. Most of the time she didn't bother to scold me when I got home and even though I still had the dinner dishes to deal with, as long as nothing else went wrong that night, I was happy.

My school was near a popular city square called *Largo da Estrela* ("Square of the Stars"). In this square stood an old church called Basilica da Estrela. Portugal has many cathedrals, some of which date back to the 12th century and even earlier. The Basilica da Estrela is relatively new, having been built in the 18th century. Everything about it fascinated me, its limestone exterior, its pink and black marbled interior with statues everywhere, and its four Corinthian columns at the front.

Four angel statues rise from the top of these columns, representing belief, honour, freedom and thankfulness, four things I desperately wanted in my life. Just looking at these angels compelled me to go into the church and pray. I got into the habit of visiting the basilica every evening for a few minutes before my classes started. The ancient ritual of kneeling on one of the old pews, feeling God all around, comforted me.

When my mother had been especially cruel and I feared my burden too much to bear, I went to God for help. I cried and prayed many times, asking Him to help my mother see that all I wanted was for her to love me. I needed Him to help her understand that I needed to go to school to have a decent future and take care of myself. Each time I left the church I felt as though I had been sitting with a good friend, someone who cared. I felt renewed and reassured that someday I would be fine.

Once in a while, in spite of everything she did to me and as I grew older, I actually felt sorry for my mother. My stepfather went to the pub every night after dinner, leaving her to wallow in loneliness. I often saw her go to the window and watch him leave the building as soon as the door latched closed behind him. Her expression was miserable with longing. I supposed the pain was one of the reasons she vented her anger on me.

Now and again, my mother took my siblings and me for an evening walk. As we passed the pub, she'd look in to see if he was carrying on with another woman. I overheard my mother tell her friend Amelia about a woman who had come knocking at her door, asking if she was Jaime's mother. Apparently, the woman had been having an affair with him and had been told he lived at home. I often thought my mother played the role of a servant and concubine, more than that of a life partner and now that I was growing older, I looked at our lives from different perspectives. I saw how hard she tried to please him by making sure his dinner was always ready when he got home, by the way she carefully laid out his clothes, by the expectant look on her face when he entered the kitchen after work. He never seemed to notice all these things and that was not how I envisioned a good relationship.

Sometimes they had terrible fights when he got home, often because someone at the pub had told him they'd seen my mother there, checking up on him. That's when my heart went out to her. In those times, I forgave her all she'd done to me and wished I could comfort her.

Wasn't that strange? Or was it because deep in my heart I still wanted her to love me as her daughter?

I got home from school at 9:30 at night. One evening, I was surprised to walk in the door and see my mother all dressed up and ready to go out. I babysat my siblings for the night and kept watch at the window for her return. I hoped she would get home before my stepfather did, so there wouldn't be any fighting. I had a feeling something bad was going on but it was none of my business and figured I was probably better off not knowing. After that night, she went out more and more frequently. I never knew where she was going and I didn't dare ask.

One Saturday night after he left for the pub, I watched my mother slouch with relief.

"Get your brother and sister ready, we're going out," she said.

I was excited. We rarely went on a family outing and the fact that she invited me meant she was no longer ashamed to be seen with me. Moments later she emerged from her bedroom, looking fresh and smiling. This unusual behaviour triggered my suspicion.

"You're going to meet a friend of mine," she told me, taking my half-brother's hand in hers. "I told him I had two children, so pretend you're my niece. Let's go."

"That's fine," I said, understanding my role perfectly. We left the apartment and walked to a local café where a serious looking man dressed in a blue striped suit joined us. They smiled at each other and my mother introduced us to her friend. He barely smiled as he nodded his head in our direction, so taken up with her was he. Based on the loving and sweet way they looked at each other, I got the general idea of what was going on, as I surreptitiously looked at them. They sat at one table while the three of us sat at another. They ordered coffee and the waiter brought some pastries and milk to our table. I had never seen my mother smile like this, she seemed happy to be with someone who paid attention to her.

After that evening my mother went out almost every night but only for another couple of weeks. Suddenly she stopped going out and her smiles vanished. She never volunteered any information or confided in me about what had happened, and I pretended I didn't notice her sullenness. I had enjoyed watching her be happy but, in a way, I was glad the whole thing ended. I constantly worried about my stepfather finding out and, as bad a mother as she could be, she was all I had and I didn't want him to hurt her.

The next time I stopped at the church on my way to school, I added my mother to my prayers.

One evening, about a year later, I had just finished cleaning up the kitchen while my mother played with the younger children in the living room. As usual, I heard my stepfather's heavy footsteps climbing the stairs but this time he didn't bother whistling for me to open the door. He used his key and headed straight for the living room. Immediately after that I heard shouting and Paulo started to cry. Something was definitely wrong.

Ana came running to the kitchen, eyes wide with fear. She

looked up at me as if she were depending on me to solve the problem. I went to my bedroom because it was closer to the living room and I could hear better. Their bedroom was just on the other side of the wall.

"Don't pretend you don't know what I'm talking about. Who do you know in France that would be sending you this letter? And don't lie to me."

I couldn't hear my mother's response. I couldn't hear if she even gave one. My heart was racing. What was happening? Did her friend in the suit have something to do with this? It had been almost a year since she had introduced him to us but I could think of nothing else.

I heard a loud thump and my mother cried out as she was thrown against the wall. I had to do something. Would he go so far as to kill her? That thought filled my brain with panic. What would happen to me? I had to end this insanity so I did the only thing I thought might help my mother.

I straightened my back, gathered all my wits and courage, then walked down the hall to their bedroom. The curtain was drawn so it would be like a closed door but I didn't bother knocking, this was an emergency. I pushed the curtain aside and glanced up at them but immediately lowered my gaze. I looked long enough though, to see the shocked expressions on both their faces.

"Stop it, please," I pleaded, glancing up at them, shyly. I then took a deep breath. "Mom, I'm sorry I got you in trouble. The truth is, I met a boy who promised he'd take me to France and marry me. That is my letter. I used your name because I didn't want him to know mine."

My story barely sounded plausible. I was sixteen years old and marriage had never crossed my mind but I didn't know what else to do. Fortunately, it seemed to work. My mother's jaw dropped in astonishment and my stepfather gaped at me as if I belonged in an asylum.

"This is insane." he declared, standing motionless as if he didn't know exactly what to do next. Then to my horror, he came towards me. At first, I thought he was going to hit me but instead, he grabbed me by the arm and dragged me towards the front door. He opened it and with his foot pushed me out onto the landing, slamming the door after me.

I sat where I fell, a little dazed. What was I supposed to do now? I doubted he would let me in if I knocked on the door.

Had I known he was going to throw me out, I would've packed a bag and thrown it out of the window beforehand. All I knew was I'd wanted him to leave my mother alone.

I waited a few minutes and when I didn't hear anything else from inside, I got up and started down the stairs.

My mother's friend, Amelia, lived up the street. I knew she and my mother confided in each other so I hoped she would help me now.

Since I had nothing but the clothes I was wearing, I didn't have many other options. I couldn't go far.

When Amelia opened the door and saw my expression, she immediately pulled me inside and asked what had happened. As I recounted all, I lost control and burst into tears, I didn't feel very brave anymore.

That evening my mother brought me some clothes to wear to work the next day. I asked her to also bring my books, which she did a short time later. I expected her to say something, something to let me know that what I did was not in vain. She said nothing.

I should have known not to expect anything from her. I'd thought she might at least acknowledge the fact that if it hadn't been for my interference, she might not be walking so straight, if at all.

Amelia gave me food and then led me to a tiny room in the next building that she sometimes rented to soldiers. An old army cot on a metal frame filled the small space as well as a sink and a toilet in a corner of the room, hidden by a curtain.

I fell asleep crying. It seemed no matter how hard I tried to do the right thing, I kept getting punished. I wondered and worried about the days to come. I couldn't stay in this tiny room forever and I didn't know what I would do if my stepfather decided not to allow me back in the apartment.

The following day when I got to work, Mrs. Santos asked me what was the matter with me. I guess I must've looked pretty sad.

"We don't have another bedroom, as you know, otherwise I would ask you to stay here for a while."

A look of horror must've crossed my face.

"What? Are you okay? Do you feel sick?" she asked concerned. I shook my head and sat on my little stool to do the work she had assigned to me.

The following days were sad but the nights in the little room were the hardest. I spent hours trying to think of some way to get myself out of this mess but no solutions came to mind. I washed my stockings and underwear in the little sink every night, then hung them over the curtain so they would be dry by morning. Then I sat on the edge of the bed and prayed, as the tears came.

After two weeks, I still had not heard from my family so I had no idea how things were going at home. One evening, there was a knock on my door and there stood my sister Ana with Amelia right behind her.

"You can come home now," she said as she stepped up to me and put her arms around my neck. "I don't know what you did to get kicked out but Mama says you can come home now,"

I collected my few belongings and left with my sister. As we climbed the stairs to the third floor, I kept wondering what would happen. Would I be punished?

From the moment I walked into the apartment, nothing was mentioned. My mother kept her silence and my stepfather returned to treating me as if I were invisible. I never discovered who wrote that letter to my mother, though I was fairly sure it was the man we had met. I didn't know what the letter was about and I didn't care. Soon the whole episode had been forgotten.

I continued going to school, always stopping beforehand at the church to pray. I put my heart and soul into those prayers, I wanted to be somebody one day. To be able to stand on my own two feet and not become a bitter, unproductive person like my mother. I prayed for God to watch over me and send some happiness my way. I prayed I would someday get away from my mother and Mr. Santos, and go somewhere I belonged and was loved.

I prayed for a future without tears

Chapter Eight

The Key to a Future

For some time, I had wanted to learn English. I thought a second language would give me a chance at getting a better job. Sometimes when I shopped for Mrs. Santos, I noticed English-speaking people coming into the stores. I stood and listened as the employees interacted with them. I tried to envision myself working in such stores, but for that, I would need to learn the language.

The local newspaper carried an ad for a correspondence course but because my mother took all my wages, I couldn't afford to take it. Even if I saved all my tips, it would have taken me years to collect all the necessary money. So, I approached the subject the next Sunday, while she was in the kitchen preparing dinner.

"Mom, would it be possible for you to lend me some money?" I asked.

She turned and looked at me suspiciously. "What do you want the money for?"

"Well, I was thinking about enrolling in an English correspondence course."

The suspicious look turned to surprise but she didn't reply, she just turned away from me and continued with her work. I went back to my room because I knew I wouldn't get anywhere today and, in a way, I was afraid she would refuse me and crush my dreams. I would wait for a better opportunity, perhaps when she was in a better mood or I could afford to buy her a present.

To my surprise, though, the next day she came to my room and told me she had decided to ask my stepfather if he would lend me the money to pay for the correspondence course. I couldn't believe my ears. What changed? Did she like me now? Were we going to be a normal family?

When my stepfather got home from work that day, he and my mother talked for a long time in the living room. I tried to listen to the conversation from my room but their voices were too muffled. After a while, I heard him and my mother pass by in the corridor and head to the kitchen. A few seconds later my mother moved my curtain aside and said, "He wants to talk with you. Get out here."

Hesitantly, I followed her, hoping this was good news.

My stepfather stood in the middle of the kitchen, stern-looking as always but standing tall, legs apart and hands on hips. He looked straight into my eyes and there was a certain inquiring softness, or curious kindness, in his look.

"Your mother tells me you want to learn English," he said. "I'm not about to waste money on this course if you won't work hard at it."

Until that moment, I had never before looked him straight in the eyes because he scared me. Now, I looked directly at him.

"I would appreciate your help and I will do my best to learn, I promise.

"What do you intend to do with this course?"

I swallowed and kept looking directly at him. "Someday, I hope to find a good job where a second language will help me get ahead."

He frowned and tilted his head but after a few seconds and as if magic, a hint of a smile played on the corners of his lips and he nodded. I waited, standing very still and hardly breathing.

"You can send for the course; I will pay for it. There is no need for you to worry about paying me back, just don't make me regret it. I'm going to trust you to keep your word and work hard at bettering yourself."

I let myself breathe. Was it my imagination or did I perceive a note of pride in his voice?

"Thank you so much." I replied with sincerity. I wanted to give him a hug but he probably would not return it so I just stayed in the same spot, trying to absorb what had just happened and wanting to jump for joy. Wow, I was going to learn English and I had their permission to do so. I felt blessed and hoped this feeling would carry on and be the end of all animosities. After they had gone back to the living room, I had to restrain myself from breaking out into song and dance all around the kitchen.

Well, I did do a little dance, quietly and in private.

One day shortly after that wonderful episode, my mother sent me to the grocery store and asked me to check the mailbox on the way back. Among the few pieces of mail, I noticed a letter from Aunt Licinia, now living in Canada with her family. My mother never went to school so she never learned to read or write. When my aunt wrote, she knew that either my stepfather or I would read her letters to my mother and also respond to her.

I started to read and she settled in to listen.

My dear sister,

I hope all is well with you and Jaime and the little ones. I miss you so much, I see myself in this land where I don't know anyone and I miss my family. It's been three years since I left but I still don't have many friends. I met our neighbours who are also Portuguese and so we interact and have become friends, which takes some of my loneliness away.

Speaking of family, dear sister, how is Lourdes? Has she gotten used to living in the city? As you know, I have always been very fond of your oldest daughter and I wish I could see her. Would you consider letting her come to

Canada and live with me? I promise you
I would take good care of her and she
would probably like it here as well. It
would make me very happy to have her
here with me.

What do you say, Angelina? Will
you think about it?

Your sister who loves very much,

Licinia

I set the letter on my lap and looked at my mother, still not believing what I'd just read. Canada? What an opportunity. My mother frowned, looking puzzled. Obviously, this had come as a shock to her as well. She stood up and started to leave the room then said over her shoulder, "We'll talk about this later."

Later? I wanted to talk about it now. I wanted a miracle to happen and have my mother tell me that I could go and live in Canada.

But I better not push my luck, I better not mention anything now and let her think about it first, I will find the right moment to approach the subject later. I sat alone, holding the letter and beaming with excitement. It would take a lot of work to convince my mother to let me go, but I was going to try. This was my future and proof that my prayers were being answered.

From the day Aunt Licinia's letter arrived, I was filled with hope. My new dreams were of Canada, a world unknown to me but one that filled me with hope. The hope of living a wonderful life independent of my mother and especially Mr. Santos, who still abused me on a regular basis. I dreamt of being free in body and spirit, of not having to worry about being defiled by any man, I dreamt of studying hard and becoming someone who had respect and dignity.

But if I were to escape all this, if I were to obtain all this, I would need my mother's permission and of that, I could never be certain. Overnight, I became the perfect, most obedient daughter on the face of the earth. When she was rude to me, I didn't get upset, I smiled instead. If she had a chore to do, I offered to do it for her. I often bought her gifts, as often as I could with the little money I had. I even started calling her "Mommy."

Making my mother happy was imperative. It would make the difference between going to Canada or staying in my present situation. Now that I had a possible avenue of escape, I couldn't bear to stay one day longer than I had to. In Canada and with my aunt's help, my opportunities will be endless, no one to stop me from finding my happiness.

I kept up the charade of being the happy and dutiful daughter but it was one very special gift that tipped the scales in my favour. My mother had been living with my stepfather since I was a small child, she had borne his children, taken care of him and his house, but they had never married. She didn't have a wedding band like all the other wives and everyone knew their status. Well, I couldn't change that but I could bring some happiness into my mother's life. I bought her a plain wedding band. I had not given her a gift in a while because I had to save every penny, but I finally did it.

When I brought the ring home one night, my mother was so overwhelmed by emotion I thought she was going to cry. That evening she was more amiable than I had ever seen her. After I'd cleaned the kitchen that night, I went into the living room and told her I thought it was an excellent idea for me to go to Canada.

"After all," I said calmly, "I've heard people make a lot of money there. And if I make a lot of money, I could send you lots of it."

She seemed composed and still admiring her gift, but I knew I had to act now, while she was feeling happy. I could tell by the look on her face she was seriously considering it and I could hardly breathe. I knew money had to be the key word.

"Mommy, you know the Canadian dollar is powerful against our escudos. When I find a job there, I will be able to send you so much more money than you get from me now. You'll be able to buy whatever you want because I will always send you money, Mommy, I will always take care of you."

I wasn't sure that I was getting through to her but her silence and the way she was attentively listening to me while slipping the ring on her finger and admiring it, gave me hope. I didn't know what else to say without repeating myself so I just waited for her response.

"Go ahead and respond to your aunt's letter, I will let you go and live with her in Canada."

I detected a bit of what I thought was sadness in her voice as she said this, but I didn't have the chance to say anything else because she just turned away from me to focus on my siblings, so I left the room.

That night I couldn't sleep. I tossed and turned in my bed wondering what my future would be like from now on. I decide to get up and bring Grandma's crucifix out of the drawer where I hid it from my mother, and pressed the old wood to my heart. I closed my eyes and thanked God for shining some light into my life, I thanked my grandmother for always being there for me, even now, I was sure. As I walked to work the next day, my feet were as light as my thoughts. I was walking on a cloud, daydreaming about Canada.

Chapter Nine

Packing My Bags

My correspondence course arrived and I enthusiastically dug in to my studies of the English language. I carried my English book wherever I went. Fortunately, since I travelled a lot by streetcar as I went to work and did my deliveries, I had a lot of study time. I practiced English everywhere, repeating words to myself, trying to string them together to construct sentences. If I thought I had made a mistake, I got out my book and corrected myself. I loved the English language and the possibilities it offered.

My aunt wrote and told us all the papers were in order, all I had to do now was wait for the Canadian embassy to call me for an interview.

Most remarkable, as my departure time approached, my mother became kinder than she had ever been. For the first time she treated me as if I were a real person and I actually began to like her. For my eighteenth birthday, she gave me a box of candy and asked if I would like her to buy me a gold chain.

I tried to smile as a knot formed in my throat and looked up at her, sadness clearly etched on my face.

"Thank you very much but I don't need a gold chain," I said simply, accepting the box of sweets.

She reached out as if to touch me but then withdrew her hand, covering her mouth with it as if to hold back tears. She looked at me with sadness and I thought I perceived regret as well in her look, then she turned and left the room.

In the past, when I would arrive home from school in the evening, I still had to wash the dinner dishes and clean the kitchen. Now when I got home, the kitchen was already clean and she had done all the housework as well. It boggled my mind. How I wished we could have had this sort of relationship from the very beginning.

A month after my eighteenth birthday I received all my papers to go to Canada.

I had my picture taken for my passport and for the Canadian government, then went to the embassy to have the final interview with a Canadian representative. I battled my nerves as I was ushered into the interview room where I met Mr. Dias who would decide my fate. He didn't speak a word of Portuguese or at least he pretended not to. I thought he could probably tell by my face that I was nervous, though I kept telling myself I could do it. After the introductions, he asked me to sit in a chair across from him.

"So, you want to go to Canada," he said, leafing through my papers.

"Yes, I do, sir.

"Who's going with you?"

"No one, Just me."

"That's very brave, going to a country far away and leaving your parents here. Aren't you going to miss them?"

"No, sir, I am not." I wanted to say. But instead I shrugged and said nothing.

"What are your expectations and what do you plan to do with yourself when you live in Canada?"

I didn't understand what he meant; my English wasn't very good yet. "Excuse me, can you repeat that?"

He spoke into his phone and a few seconds later, his secretary came into the room. He repeated to her what he had asked me and she translated.

"Senhor Dias quer que tu lhe digas o que tu pensas que o Canada vai fazer por ti, que Portugal nao esta a fazer. Como ves o teu futuro no Canada?"

I wanted my answer to be clear and precise so Mr. Dias would know that going to Canada meant the world to me.

"I want to go to Canada to study and to work. I think Canada has more opportunities for me than Portugal," I said as I sat up straight and hoped my message was clear enough.

Mr. Dias nodded to the woman and she left the room. He sat back in his chair and seemed to be appraising me, perhaps wondering why a young woman like me wanted to run away from her family and her country.

I returned his gaze and speculated what his answer might be. Was he going to say I couldn't go? He couldn't do that; I would get down on my knees and beg for my freedom, if necessary.

He stood up and extended his hand to me.

"Congratulations, Miss Maria de Lourdes Almeida," he said, reading my name from the papers in his hand. "Your application is now approved and you can go to Canada. I need you to go through some health tests but I'm sure you will pass those as well."

He smiled as I shook his hand. He must've seen the tears in my eyes but I didn't care, he had just opened a door for me and I would walk through it with confidence, I was so happy.

"Goodbye and good luck."

"Goodbye, Mr. Dias, and thank you."

The secretary smiled at me and waved as I walked calmly past her desk while in my head, I was doing a little dance.

I went to see the doctors I was referred to the following week and passed with flying colours. All I had to do now was wait for my ticket which my wonderful Aunt Licinia had already paid for, to arrive from Canada.

By the end of August, I was still anxiously waiting for my passport to arrive so Mrs. Santos suggested to her husband that they distract me by taking me on a day trip around Portugal before I left it for good. She knew I had never been anywhere other than Lisbon and Granja.

The thought of accepting anything from this man whom I loathed absolutely repulsed me, but his wife had always been good to me. I focused my thoughts on enjoying a bit of the country I had never been fortunate enough to know, except through books. I have to admit that I was relieved to learn Deolinda and her husband—yes, she was a married woman—had decided to come with us.

They took us to Santarem where Portugal's first king, Afonso Henriques, was born in the eleventh century. Santarem is perched on the west bank of the river Tagus, north of Lisbon, overlooking the pasturelands where most of Portugal's bulls are bred for its famous bullfights.

After Santarem, we went to the city of Fatima, the point of pilgrimage for millions of Roman Catholics. One of the most important religious shrines in the Catholic world is in that city.

Once a tiny village, Fatima was transformed in 1917 when three young children experienced six visions of the blessed Virgin. Since then, millions of people flock to the site every year, many making the journey on foot from neighbouring villages. I knelt by the shrine and prayed to God that my adventure to Canada would be a happy one. I also prayed for my mother, asking God to bless her and look after her. It was strange but her recent kindness left me feeling a little melancholy. I held no grudges against her but at the same time, I'd be happy to go away and never come back.

From Fatima we travelled to Nazareth where we stopped at a restaurant for lunch. The first things the waitress brought us were olives, fresh bread, and a large carafe of red wine. It was so typically Portuguese that I vowed to come back for a visit someday and stop at restaurants such as this one. The food and the ambiance were the best I had ever seen, even though I had not seen much. When the server set the plate in front of me, my mouth watered. A steak, surrounded by the most delicious looking French fries and crowned by an over-easy egg, just about took my breath away as I picked up my knife and fork. All this, the view of the Atlantic, and the Portuguese ballads playing on a Victrola in a corner of the room, made up a memory I would remember for the rest of my life.

After feasting, we walked across the street and took our shoes off so we could walk on the white sand beach and watch the fishermen bring in their catch.

I was exhausted at the end of the day but also happy and enlightened by everything I'd seen and learned. What a thrill to have visited so many amazing sites.

The next day I went to the travel agency to set my departure date. I booked my trip to Canada for October 30, 1971, just over one week away. Two days later, I was thrilled to pick up all the necessary paperwork as well as my passport from the Canadian Embassy.

Despite my happiness, I was well aware that in the coming week anything could happen. I wouldn't even have been surprised if my mother decided to change her mind. She could get angry at me for whatever reason and destroy all my documents so, as a precaution, I hid everything under my bed and I behaved impeccably, keeping her happy.

The day before I left, I felt sick with conflicting emotion. This was my deliverance, the day I had dreamed about since I could remember. I was deliriously happy to be leaving and yet ... I wished I had been happier in Portugal. I wished it hadn't been necessary for me to run to another country to better my life.

My stepfather drove my mother, my siblings and me to the airport, and my mother cried all the way there. Maybe she regretted the things she had done to me. Maybe she was actually going to miss me. I couldn't tell. But I couldn't allow my emotion to take control so before I said goodbye, I put my arm around her shoulders and asked her to be happy for me. I told her I wouldn't forget her and would try to send her money, always.

When the loudspeaker announced it was time to board, I walked to the gate with confidence. Before I turned the corner, I gave a final wave, then left my past behind.

Part Two

Canada

Chapter Ten

Deliverance

Is home the place where we first physically arrive? Or is it a place we carve out for ourselves? I believe it's a place where we discover we're not afraid anymore, where we always feel safe and protected, where we feel free to love and be loved, and where we can enjoy an infinite playground with no hidden agendas or cruelty.

Up until the minute I left the country where I was born, I was a wanderer. Displaced, unsure of the future, and very, very lonely. Now as the plane neared Canada, most of those feelings lifted. Although the uncertainty of the future was still there, I instinctively felt I belonged in this part of the world. Here was where I would begin carving out my home.

When the pilot announced we would be landing in Toronto in a few minutes, I could hardly contain my excitement. I looked out the window at my new country. It was six a.m., still a little dark and nothing was very discernible, but the feeling of home engulfed me. I was here, I was where I was supposed to be, nothing else mattered anymore.

Walking through the terminal towards Customs, I couldn't believe I was finally here. My nightmare life with my mother and Mr. Santos was finally over, forever.

The Customs Officer asked some questions but after looking through my papers and seeing they were in order, he smiled and welcomed me to Canada. I smiled back, thanked him, then moved towards the exit. I was jubilant.

Floor-to-ceiling glass windows separated me from the waiting area. As I neared them, I surveyed the faces on the other side of the glass and located my family, waving and smiling at me. They were all there: Aunt Licinia, Uncle Roberto, and my cousins, Roger, Pedro, and little Sabrina. When I stepped into the waiting area, it was like I stepped into an entirely different world. And it *was* a different world.

Everyone hugged and kissed me and I'm sure I must have thanked my aunt and uncle a thousand times in those first few moments, for giving me this opportunity. I was so happy and filled with gratitude for my new freedom. Once we were all together in the car, my cousins became quiet and shy. Aside from my aunt's endless chit-chat, there weren't many questions being asked. I didn't mind. I was happy to have the time to look out the window. Lisbon is an old city, old buildings with stores embedded on the lower levels. This city looked modern but strangely old in a different way. Some buildings were covered with graffiti and people walked as if carrying the weight of the world on their shoulders. I also saw some very tall buildings, taller that I had ever seen in Portugal. All these things were new to me but I embraced the idea of living here, of making this my home.

On the way to their house, Uncle Roberto stopped and bought my first meal in my new country, fried chicken with potato salad. He carried the bags into the house and we all sat together to enjoy what I thought was a most delicious meal. No more leftovers for me.

After dinner, I had to answer all their questions about how everyone was in Portugal. I enhanced the truth a lot because I didn't want to start my new life in Canada with people feeling sorry for me. So, I told them everything was fine, everyone was doing well.

Before going to bed, I kissed my aunt and uncle goodnight, and thanked them again for bringing me here.

It took a long, long time for me to fall asleep, even though I was exhausted after all the travelling. I still couldn't believe I was really in Canada. I felt so happy and thankful to be with relatives who were good to me. I vowed I would do my best to deserve their love, to learn the language, follow the customs and be a good citizen of this country that had received me with open arms.

By November, I was familiar with the routine of my new home and loved my new family. Sabrina was a typical little girl who desperately wanted a sister to play with. Pedro was a bit aloof but pleasant, and Roger liked to have fun and would do anything to get a girl's attention. I was the oldest, so I felt as if I had become the older sister to them all.

In the first few days, my aunt took me shopping at Towers, a local department store where she bought me a dress that reached my feet as well as a pair of moccasins for me to wear around the house. This store was also different from the stores in Portugal. There, merchandise was kept behind counters and most of the time in drawers. Employees brought out whatever you asked for. Here, you could touch and hold everything, no one looked over your shoulder and when you were done, you just took it to the cashier and paid for it.

I discovered that we lived in an area called Downsview, in a spacious modern house with two floors and a basement. To me, it was a castle. I no longer had to wash my clothes in an old tub over a scrubbing board, I could let a washing machine do it for me. Aunt Licinia explained what detergents to use and how to operate the machine. The floors didn't need to be scoured with an old brush and yellow soap because they were linoleum. My aunt had something called a mop, which she used to clean the floor. Amazing.

I shared my bedroom with Sabrina and we had an actual door that we could close, not just a curtain. Even more amazing.

Both their toilet and their shower were in a private room, separated from the rest of the house by a door. The first time I took a shower in my relatives' home, I stayed in it for a very long time, relishing the flow of hot water over my body.

Aside from the odd chore, all I did was play with my cousins and go shopping with my aunt. I felt totally spoiled but I was so used to hard work that all this leisure made me uneasy at times. My new life seemed too good to be true and I feared I might have to suffer the consequences of my good fortune sometime later. I kept asking my aunt to let me do chores for her but she just smiled and told me to enjoy myself. So, I did! I felt free and joyous. The healing of my soul began.

Both my aunt and my cousin Roger attended evening classes to improve their English. When I asked if I could go with them, my uncle shook his head. He told me I would soon be in school full time and that came as a shock, too. For once, someone had taken my best interests to heart without my asking.

Although it was only November, it was cold in Canada compared to Portugal. My aunt warned me the impending winter would get even colder. She said she would have to buy me some warm clothes or I would freeze to death. My uncle didn't work on Fridays so after dinner one Thursday evening, they took me to Towers again where they bought me a coat, gloves, and a scarf.

I knew I would repay them for it all someday, but how is it possible to repay the feeling of being loved and cared for? I couldn't find the words to describe the warm, fuzzy feeling my aunt gave me, as she stood in the department store holding my coat so I could try it on.

"Do you like it?" she asked, looking concerned.

I beamed at her. "Like it? I love it."

It took a few days before my uncle found an appropriate school for me to attend. The one he chose was specifically for new Canadians and it was in Toronto. We were told I could start any time so, of course, I wanted to begin right away. On the way home, my uncle stopped and bought school supplies for me and handed me a five-dollar bill.

"This is your weekly allowance," he said, answering my look of bewilderment.

"Thank you so much. This is very kind of you," I said.

"That's all you're getting, so don't squander it." My uncle said. I felt bad taking his money because he sounded like he didn't want to part with it

Chapter Eleven

Learning Again

A mixed feeling of euphoria and awkwardness assailed me as I
entered the classroom for the first time. I didn't know anyone. Then I
remembered the people in this school were all new Canadians, just
like me, so I relaxed a bit. The teacher, Mrs. Hawkins, a lovely
woman in her thirties, welcomed me into the class and introduced
me to everyone as the new student. Everyone smiled and waved at
me, making me feel at ease. The diversity in people was interesting
and new. People of all ages who were there for the same reason as
me, to become a part of this country and to have a better life here
than we had in our own countries. I loved it and felt the warmth in
everyone and it wasn't long before they all bombarded me with

questions that I struggled to understand. So many accents. So many voices.

"Where you from?"

"Are you here with your parents?"

"Are your parents coming to you?

"So hard, you leave your parents in Portugal. You miss them?"

I just answered the questions but I didn't engage in explanations why I didn't miss my parents or why it wasn't hard at all to leave them behind. I thought that if I told anyone the truth about my life back in Lisbon, they might not be so friendly with me and I wanted to make friends.

"You have brothers and sisters?"

"Are they in Portugal with your parents or here with you?"

"You came to Canada alone? You so brave."

I couldn't tell if the last comment was made out of admiration or pity but I smiled and told them as best as I could in my limited English that it had been a great adventure and that I was very happy with my new family. They didn't ask any more questions after that and I was relieved to no longer be the centre of attention.

After the awkwardness of the first day I became just another student and, to my relief, I actually felt as if I belonged. Since every student was a new immigrant, it could be a challenge sometimes trying to communicate through body language and broken phrases. The mood in the classroom was comfortable and supportive. We helped each other as much as we could and no one was offended when one classmate corrected another.

My English improved quickly but I still had a long way to go. I bought a newspaper every morning and read all the stories, but I also carried a small dictionary with me, in case I had to look up a word I didn't understand. Just like in Lisbon when I took my books in the streetcar, my bus trips to and from school became a perfect place to learn, as I had no distractions.

The class went on field trips to interesting places such as Niagara-on-the-Lake and Niagara Falls, learning about this new country of ours. On this trip, I made friends with a girl from China who was also at the school to better her English.

Helen and I got along so well that we became fast friends. The next week we went on a guided tour of the Parliament buildings in Ottawa, and Helen and I stayed together and learned together. We did the pinkie promise that we would stay friends even after we left school. Both as eager to learn the language as we could've been, we helped each other all the time. I constantly asked questions and sponged up the answers, filling my head with knowledge, wanting to learn as much as I could, and so did Helen. I missed her when summer break started and I didn't see her everyday.

Not going to school afforded me a lot of time with my aunt and her family. She worked nights picking worms so she slept all day and I helped by cooking and cleaning. One day, she suggested I come with her to pick worms. Apparently worm picking was a job many students took up in the summer because it was easy money. For their immigrant parents, it was the ideal job as well, as most of them didn't speak English and the worms didn't care what language you spoke. I concluded that this was a good opportunity for me to make some money and perhaps keep my promise to my mother. When my aunt told me that I would get paid $7.50 for every 500 worms I picked, I almost changed my mind. How long would it take me to pick 500 worms?

Just after dusk one day, a van stopped in front of our house to pick us up. I could see two men in the front seats.

When we climbed in, eight people sitting on the floor in the back had to shift over and make room for us. They were all Portuguese, men and women. I couldn't help thinking we were like cattle, all corralled together in that small space.

When my aunt's fellow worm pickers heard this was my first time, they all assured me there was nothing to it.

"Picking worms is a piece of cake," someone said.

"Just keep thinking it's money you're picking and you will feel much better."

At that, someone giggled and I was soon listening to stories about worm picking. I didn't know anyone and introductions were not made, so I just listened.

"Remember the day Fatima and Jack were late and the driver wanted to leave?" Someone asked no one in particular.

"Oh boy do I ever," someone responded. "I think they got carried away and it wasn't worms they were picking."

"Yeah, they were pecking at each other," someone else said, laughing. All of a sudden everyone was laughing, including me.

When we arrived at the golf course where we were to pick these worms, the grass was silvery grey under a full moon and you could see forever, but it wasn't long before some large grey clouds moved in. Soon, everyone was getting ready to start and as I looked around for my aunt, I glimpsed her going into the field. I watched her go and felt a moment's panic as darkness engulfed her. I had no idea where to find her afterwards.

A man handed me two large cans that had held coffee in better days. One of the cans was filled with sawdust and the other was empty. I was also given two rubber bands to secure the cans around my legs and a miner's light to put on my forehead so I could see the worms. I asked what the sawdust was for and the man told me if I dipped my hand in it, it would make it easier to hold the worm so it wouldn't get away.

It all sounded revolting but I couldn't turn back now, I was there to make money and nothing was going to stop me. When I had secured the cans just below my knees, the man told me to go out and start collecting. He said when I had a full can it meant I had five hundred worms and at that point, I was to drop them off at the van and then start all over again.

I walked away from the man and into the dark of the night, not seeing anyone. I could hear the distant talking and laughter of some of the people working in groups but as I walked farther along, all I heard was the pounding of my heart.

Despite my apprehension, I kept going into the darkness, looking for worms. The memory of a much younger me walking the cattle home from pasture in the dark came to mind, but I immediately dismissed it, focussing instead on how much money I was going to make, or not, this night. I didn't feel brave but I tried to talk myself into believing I could do it. This was going to be the first money I would earn in my new country and I had to be courageous.

It took me a long time to pick my first worm. I shone the light on the ground and saw some but as soon as I got closer, they disappeared back into the underground. I could see I would never get any if they always hid when I spotted them. I looked over my shoulder, wondering how the other people caught the slippery things but all I could see were dim lights far, far away. I guessed the other pickers must be quick as lightning because these worms weren't going to wait around to get caught once the light shone on them.

I pondered my problem for a while, glancing around to see if I could spot someone who could tell me how to do this strange job. I was alone. I could try to find the van by going back the same way I had come, but I was disoriented and had no idea in which direction to go. I looked up, wishing the moon would come out from behind the clouds and give me a little help but it seemed to be pretty well hidden for the time being. I would have to solve this problem on my own, then worry about finding the van when the can was full. I figured that would probably take me all night.

I was so frustrated; the worms were quicker than me. Or, maybe they just didn't like light. After all, there had to be a reason why they stayed underground all day and only came out at night.

I squatted and tried to keep the ray of light pointed a few inches ahead by tilting my head slightly upwards. I kept my eyes directed at the ground close to my feet, and I felt both nauseated and amazed when I finally witnessed a worm slithering halfway out of its hole and onto the cool grass.

Now I had to pick it up. I touched the dew-wet grass beside me then dipped my fingers in the can containing sawdust. With a quick move I tried to grab the worm, but it must have still had a good grip on the earth below because suddenly, I found myself holding only half a worm. Disgusted, I threw the thing away from me and wiped my hand on the grass again.

But I didn't give up. The next time, I waited until the worm was entirely out of its hole, then I dipped my hand in the sawdust again and plucked up the worm with my thumb and forefinger. I held it away from me. I didn't want to look at it because I knew I'd feel either sick, or sorry for it. I dropped the worm into the can, feeling repulsed. I had never been in a situation when I actually had to touch a worm and even with the sawdust, it still felt wet and slimy. I was tempted to go back to the van and tell the man this was definitely not the job for me, but then I remembered I could use the money. I had to learn how to do this correctly.

I decided to use a lot more sawdust so they wouldn't feel so slippery. I had been told I wouldn't be paid for broken worms so after I'd thrown away a few, I got the hang of it. I learned how to trap the worm as it emerged from the hole then slowly ease it out. It took forever to catch one and that was frustrating. I had only two worms in the can but it seemed as if I had been out there all night.

And then it got easier. I pulled up whole worms and before I knew it, the can was full. I stood up and scanned around me but I had no idea which way to get back to the van. Now that the clouds had passed, I used moonlight to find shadows in the distance, so I walked in their direction. The full can was heavy on my leg but I didn't bother taking it off. If I had to carry it, I'd smell the contents and I definitely did not want to do that.

I spotted a light on someone's head as they hurried by some distance away and I called out. It was my aunt. She was on her way back to unload her pickings. I followed her but had a hard time keeping up with her quick gait due to the weight on my legs.

When she asked how many worms I had picked, I proudly said, "Five hundred."

I couldn't see the expression on her face but suddenly she was walking faster and that told me she was disappointed.

"You mean this is your first can?" she finally called back. "I have picked five thousand so far. Before the night is over, I will have doubled that."

I didn't know what to say. I thought I had done pretty well but not according to my aunt. I would have to get better.

The same man took my full can and poured the worms into a shallow wooden box, then spread them with his hand to check for broken ones. Satisfied, he gave the can back. "You've done a good job." At least someone appreciated my efforts.

By four in the morning my back ached and I shivered with cold. Then the rain came.

My second can was only half full when it started but then something amazing happened. As it rained, the worms crawled out of their holes and there were so many I hardly had to move. I picked up handfuls of them with no problem. I ran to the truck, then went back to fill another can while the pickings were good. I filled my fourth can but by then my clothes had been wet so long I was shivering miserably. I went back and asked if I could sit in the van until it was time to go. The man nodded.

I sat shivering in the van for hours, wondering when the other people would come back. I wished I was home in my warm bed. I found an old blanket in a corner of the van and wrapped myself in it, trying to get the chill out of my bones. I decided if I was going to do this for a living, I had better buy myself a raincoat.

It was 6:30 a.m. when everyone returned. Needless to say, they were happy to have had such a wonderful and rainy night. My aunt bragged about picking fifteen thousand worms but her tone and manner seemed somewhat accusatory when she looked in my direction. I just wanted to go home.

"How did you do tonight?" she asked me.

"Two thousand." I replied, looking at her and wanting her approval.

"Two thousand?" she repeated then shook her head. "You've got to work hard in order to succeed in this business and you're not going to make any money sitting in the van." She turned to her friends and away from me.

I was shocked. What brought on that attitude? It was as if a nasty blanket of criticism engulfed me and, for the first time in a very long while, I thought of my mother. I felt cold and miserable enough and my aunt should have been more understanding. It was my first night and I'd done pretty well, considering no one had given me any lessons. And I was proud to have earned thirty dollars. It was the most money I'd ever had.

The following day, as I had promised, I put ten dollars in an envelope and sent it to my mother.

Every muscle in my body ached and I could hardly move. I didn't want to eat or talk or do anything else. I declined the offer to go worm picking the next night because I knew I would never be a successful worm picker. Instead, I vowed to study hard and get a good job so I wouldn't ever be forced to pick worms for a living. I went back to cooking and cleaning the house.

Chapter Twelve

A Woman's Place

The following weekend we went to a party in a nearby town. It was an annual Portuguese picnic and everybody knew each other except me, of course, but I didn't mind going because I wanted to interact with other Portuguese people.

I came to the picnic to be with others, yet sat off by myself, deep in thought. I sensed trouble in our house and I didn't know what to do.

For some reason, my aunt wasn't in a very good mood that day, either. In fact, she hadn't been in a good mood for a while. It seemed as if I was the problem but I had no idea what I had done to make her angry. She no longer smiled when she talked with me and if I asked a question, her answer was always curt. At first, I thought she was just having a bad day but it continued for weeks. She was pleasant to everyone else but as soon as I came into the picture, her demeanour turned cold and indifferent. This made me sad; it was a true echo of life back in Portugal. I wondered why she had asked me to come to Canada in the first place. Everything had been so pleasant when I first arrived but now, I'd become like an intruder in her home.

The last time I'd seen my aunt—before I came to Canada—I'd been a young child living with my grandparents. She had always been very protective and I imagined she'd felt sorry for me when I was moved to Lisbon and into my mother's house. Now, I wondered what she was thinking and why things had become so uncomfortable between us. I had changed a lot since coming to Canada. I had shed the protective mantle I had been forced to wear all my life, and was now relaxed, happy and outgoing. Maria de Lourdes was popular, especially with people my own age and with my cousins. I didn't know if that was the reason for my aunt's resentment but I could think of no other.

I was no longer the little girl she remembered but that was hardly my fault. I couldn't help comparing myself to a plant that had been kept in a dark room. When that plant is taken into the sunlight and watered, it thrives and blooms, just as I did when I came to Canada. Now I thirsted for water again and there was hardly any light in my life.

I was jolted out of my reveries when my name was called. My cousins and uncle were playing soccer and since they'd noticed I was sitting by myself, they invited me to play with them. It was time for me to forget my sullen mood and have some fun.

My aunt was in animated conversation with other Portuguese women some distance away. When I looked in her direction, her face held disapproval as she watched me. At the end of the game I joined her, hoping to learn why she was in such a bad mood. When she turned to face me, her expression told me I should've stayed away.

She looked like her sister, my mother.

"Do you see any other girls playing soccer with the men?" she asked reproachfully.

"No," I replied, "but I was just playing with my uncle and cousins. I didn't think there was anything wrong with that."

"You ought to be ashamed of yourself," she scoffed, looking me up and down.

She turned abruptly and walked towards her friends, leaving me wondering what was going on in her head. I had no idea what I had done to her.

Just the week before, she had come into my bedroom in the morning to wake me. I'd opened my eyes and seen her bending over me, her expression conspiratorial. I was instantly awake.

"Lourdes," she whispered, "tell your uncle you are sick today and stay home with me."

One thing my uncle couldn't tolerate was lying. He had once told me that to be a good liar you had to have an excellent memory and I didn't fit the bill. I can't remember why he told me that, but it must have been because he thought I was lying about something. I didn't want to disappoint my aunt but I also didn't want to lie to my uncle. Besides, the thought of missing school worried me, was I destined to be kept in darkness all my life? I suggested that maybe she should be the one to tell him but she just sighed impatiently and left my room.

A few moments later my uncle stormed in, holding a thermometer in his hand. He stuck it in my mouth then sat on the bed, waiting. When he removed the thermometer and looked at it, I could see from his frown that he wasn't pleased.

"You don't have a fever so whatever you're feeling can't be too serious. Get up and get dressed, you're going to school." In spite of his gruffness, I was thankful.

When I came down from my bedroom with my books under my arm, ready to go to school, my aunt kept busy cleaning the stove. I told her I'd see her later but she didn't answer. From the accusing glare she gave me, I thought it best not to say anything else.

My uncle was already in the car waiting to take me to the subway, so I hurried outside. I was thankful the ride wasn't long because if he had questioned me about pretending to be sick, I would not have known what to say. I could never betray my aunt but I didn't want to lie. Either way I was in trouble.

Only after he'd dropped me off at the subway station did I try to analyze the situation. Why had she asked me to feign being sick? Was she that lonely that she wanted me with her? Did she not care if I got an education? Since she hadn't been particularly kind to me lately, I even had to wonder what exactly her motives were for wanting me to come to Canada.

Was I supposed to become a companion and stay home with her all day? I hadn't spent much time alone with her but I hadn't thought she wanted that. My heart ached when I realized the probable reason for my aunt's attitude. If I had been brought to Canada to keep her company, I had failed miserably. I had been so busy fulfilling my own needs and feeling liberated that I'd hardly spent any time with her. Based on that, she most likely had the impression that I was arrogant, thoughtless and ungrateful.

Now, as Aunt Licinia walked away from me to be with the other women at the picnic, it all made sense. She didn't want me playing and having fun with everyone else because she wanted me to sit with her. I didn't know what to do. I certainly didn't want to be on her bad side. I loved her, but I wished I knew the reason she was resenting me so I could fix it. Tears filled my eyes threatening to spill and I had to struggle to keep my emotions under control so as not to draw attention to myself. I supposed I should try to be more like the other women, sitting and gossiping. That was what they were doing at that moment, only this time, I was painfully aware that I was the subject of their disapproval. One woman made a point of raising her voice and when I looked their way, I saw her pointing a finger in my direction. She held my gaze, making sure I heard what she had to say.

"You're absolutely right to be angry, Dona Licinia. Imagine the ungrateful girl, playing with the men and totally ignoring you. She should be sitting with us and behaving like a lady. Did you say her mother beat her? Well, why am I not surprised?"

I didn't understand the way these women's minds worked. All they did was eat, drink, and gossip. The men played with the children but the women did nothing. Because of what the woman had said, I now felt resentful towards my aunt's friends. They certainly weren't making matters any better between my aunt and me. Who knew what other ideas they were putting in her head? My uncle and cousins continued playing soccer, laughing and yelling, oblivious to the turmoil going on around them. I sat and watched them, smiling occasionally but otherwise feeling gloomy. They tried to get me up to play with them again but I shook my head. I was determined to sit there and behave like a lady, even if it killed me.

Maybe if my aunt noticed I wasn't having any fun, she would change her mind and be a little kinder towards me.

I hadn't meant to upset her but when I was chasing the ball, I felt good.

I promised myself I would mend my ways and do my best to make my aunt like me again. Maybe not today but in the future. The afternoon ended with a lot of tension all around because by now, everyone knew Licinia was not happy.

For the next few days, I tried to put aside my own needs and paid more attention to my aunt. I worked hard at observing my surroundings and the behaviour of people around me more carefully.

When school started again that fall, I was relieved to have some distraction other than staying at home and wondering what would happen that day. I was glad to see Helen again, too, and we had a great time going to the movies with the teacher and the rest of the class to see "Play it Again, Sam". I struggled to follow the dialogue but I understood enough to know what the movie was all about. Helen and I discussed the story afterwards and giggled about the funny parts, while we took a walk through the park to learn about the native plants and trees. At one point, Helen stopped me and said, "I hope you don't mind me saying this, Maria, but did you notice the way Diane Keaton walked in the movie?"

I was a little perplexed.

"You know," Helen continued, "All the great models and stars walk like this, watch."

She walked in front of me, placing one foot in front of the other while I watched with fascination and understanding. I knew I didn't walk like that, so elegant.

"You try it." Helen encouraged me with her engaging and friendly smile.

I walked in front of Helen with my head held high and doing exactly as she did. I liked it. My new way of walking. After that, I make a conscious decision to walk the way all the great models, stars, and Helen, walked. At the end of the day, I hugged my friend and thanked her for the lesson.

The boys in our school for new Canadians played soccer against other schools and Helen and I were invited to be cheerleaders. Helen graciously declined but I accepted, I thought it would be fun. I was also pleased because one of the players, a boy named Paris, had been flirting with me for some time. Tall and slim, with brown hair and light brown eyes, Paris was very popular with both male and female students. So, I joined the cheerleaders and had a wonderful time watching the games and cheering the team on. One day after a game, Paris asked if I would go out on a date with him.

Other boys from the school had asked me out, but I'd turned every one of them down because my main goal was to study, not to play around with boys. But there was something about Paris that made me blush every time he looked at me. When we were in class, I could feel his eyes on me and that gave me a pleasant feeling.

I couldn't help thinking that if I found someone and got married, I would be able to move out of my relative's house and find a life for myself. At first, I said no to his attempts of getting closer to me, but he wasn't to be discouraged. I finally agreed to let him ride on the subway with me at the end of the day. We felt comfortable in each other's company and talked all the way. When we arrived at my station, he took my hand and kissed it, telling me he liked me very much. From that day on we held hands all the time and everything felt wonderful to me. I smiled more and was happy to have someone whose company I enjoyed so much.

At the end of the school year, my English had improved tremendously. I didn't see the need to return and started thinking of getting a job. Helen wasn't returning, either. She was engaged to be married to the love of her life, Henry, a man who made her eyes light up whenever she talked about him.

On the last day of school, Paris and I took the subway together. When we got to my stop, he held my hand and asked me if I had told my family about him.

"No," I admitted.

A serious look came over his face. "Maria, I would like to get to know you better and now that we're out of school, the only way I can see you is if you go out with me."

"You know I would love to go out with you, Paris," I said. "But I live with my aunt and uncle and they are very strict."

"How about if I come and introduce myself to them?" he asked, an optimistic smile on his face.

I shook my head. "I don't think that would work. That would put them on the spot and my uncle wouldn't appreciate it."

"Does this mean I might never see you again?" he asked.

I sighed, hating to see the pain in his eyes. "Paris, give me some time to get them used to the idea of me going on a date. I promise I will call you."

He hugged me and kissed my cheek before we went our separate ways. When I got home, I told my uncle and aunt that I had met a boy and would like to go to the movies with him.

My uncle wanted to know where I had met this boy and who he was. I told him I knew Paris from school and he was a kind and respectful boy. My uncle said he'd think about it, then left it at that. I had to count that as a kind of victory, I guessed. At least he hadn't said no.

A couple of weeks later, a friend of the family, Arminda, was having a birthday party for her daughter and she invited all of us to come. I asked her if I could invite Paris to the party and she said yes.

I called him that evening and invited him.

"I would love to come, what a wonderful opportunity for me to meet your relatives," he said, sounding cheerful.

"I'm looking forward to it but don't be too disappointed if it doesn't work, my uncle is old-school and a very difficult person to deal with," I warned.

"Will you meet me at the subway station before the party? Then we can plan how to best approach your uncle," he said.

"Sure, I wish us luck."

The day of the party arrived and as promised, I met Paris at the subway station and we took the bus back. We went into the house and on to the backyard where the party was being held. I introduced Paris to my family and the people I knew best. Everyone was very polite but my uncle and aunt seemed indifferent. I sensed Paris was nervous so I stayed with him as much as I could that day. I noticed small groups of people looking in our direction and talking and I had a feeling I knew what they were saying. My family was known to them all and here I was, daring to bring a stranger into their midst.

Paris must have felt the tension, too, because in spite of his good intentions, he never spoke with my uncle about us. A short while later he told me he had to get going so I walked outside with him and told him not to worry, there would be another chance. We talked for a while outside and when I returned to the party, my uncle was talking with two men I didn't know. It made me shudder and feel vulnerable. I lowered my eyes, wishing I didn't feel as if my clothes were being stripped off me by total strangers.

"What the hell took you so long?" my uncle demanded in front of the two men. "You know I get mad easily and if I do, we are going to have problems, Lourdes."

My heart was in my throat. "I'm sorry," I said. "We just talked."

"You'd better be careful," he warned. "Your friend Paris, or whatever his name is, wasn't even man enough to talk with me."

I was intimidated at this unaccustomed anger but also annoyed with him for not trusting me. What did he expect I was doing outside in the middle of the day? I didn't understand what he might be thinking.

Later, Arminda came to me and asked if we could talk for a minute. She looked so worried I thought something horrible had happened.

"Sure," I said, then followed her upstairs to her bedroom.

"What is it?" I begged as she led me to sit on the bed beside her.

She grabbed my shoulders with both hands and looked intently at me. "Be careful, Lourdes. Your aunt and uncle are very upset, I heard them say they were going to pack your bags and send you back to Portugal."

I felt as if I'd been punched in the stomach. "Oh, my dear God." I exclaimed. "Why would they want to do that?"

"I don't know, but they're upset about something you did. I heard your uncle talking with my husband but I couldn't quite follow the whole conversation."

She looked worried about me and I assured her I wouldn't tell them what she had just told me.

I stayed outwardly calm but, in my heart, I was in turmoil. I was aware that on the contract the Canadian government had asked them to sign, they agreed to keep me for a minimum of five years. So why were they doing this? What had I done that was so serious? Were they trying to scare me to make me behave? If so, how should I be behaving?

Suddenly everything was uncertain. My life was in their hands, they had the power. I didn't think anything I said was going to be good enough so I decided the best thing to do was to wait and see what came of it. I supposed the worst thing that could happen was that I could end up in my mother's house again.

Oh, but could I survive that fate?

I didn't know what to do. I closed my eyes as our car pulled out of our friend's driveway, I prayed silently. I thought I was being good and obedient. What had I done?

No one said a word until we got home.

Chapter Thirteen

Trapped in a Maze

As soon as we got home from the party, I headed towards my bedroom but my uncle intercepted me and told me to sit in the living room.

"What gives you the right to talk badly about us to your cousin?" he demanded. "Don't we keep a roof over your head? Don't we feed you and treat you as one of our own? What makes you so ungrateful?"

I had no idea what he was talking about at the time but then he pulled out Tony's letter from his pocket. He let me know that my aunt had found it and showed it to him.

My cousin, Tony, who sometimes walked with me to bring the cows home in Granja, was in the Portuguese army. I corresponded with him because he had written to me once, telling me how lonely army life was. His mother, Filomena, didn't know how to write, like my mother, she had never gone to school, so he received few letters from home. I always hoped my letters would bring him some comfort. I told him about my life in Canada, how I loved this country and my family, but I also told him how strict my uncle was. In one of his letters, he suggested that perhaps I should consider moving out if I wasn't getting along with them.

Now I understood. I didn't ask him what right they had to go through my things, I simply sat there, took their wrath and then went to bed.

When my uncle got home from work the next day, he looked worried, tired, and pale. He went straight to his bedroom without eating and he didn't talk with anyone, even my aunt.

"What's wrong with him?" I asked.

"It's all your fault," my aunt said. "He's in this condition because of you."

I just stared at her, having no idea what she was talking about. What had I done? She told me I had worried him sick. He felt responsible for me and I had caused him grief rather than being the grateful niece.

By Friday my uncle had to see the doctor. He was told he was on the verge of a nervous breakdown, the doctor suggested he might have to go to hospital if he didn't get better. I felt horrible. By now, I was convinced he was sick because of me.

Later that same week, as he rested in his recliner, he called to me and asked me to sit on the sofa beside him.

"I'm concerned about this guy you brought to the party, what was his name?"

"Paris" I replied, not knowing where he was going with this.

"I know why Paris wants to go out with you. He wants to show you off to his friends and to use you. Is he from Greece?"

He was looking at me inquisitively so I nodded in answer to his question.

"Yeah, I know his kind. I work with a lot of Greeks and I don't like any of them. When they want to have their way with a girl, they give her things to drink and smoke and then they have their way with her."

My jaw dropped. I couldn't believe he was saying these foul things and insinuating my Paris would do this to me.

"If Paris ever does anything like that to you," my uncle continued, "I'll end up in jail but Paris will be six feet under. He won't be able to harm anyone else ever again."

I was speechless. Whatever had given him these ideas? Paris was gentle, loving, and polite to everyone. I knew my uncle was old-fashioned and I supposed he felt responsible for me, but this hurt. He should have known he could trust me, or at least give me credit for some intelligence.

"What will you do when Sabrina grows up?" my aunt piped up, coming out of the kitchen. Obviously, she had been listening to the conversation.

He crossed his arms and glared at us both. "I will do the same thing. I do for one what I would do for the other. While Lourdes is in my house, she lives by my rules." He jabbed a finger against his chest.

Wow, I suspected I was in a bit of trouble here.

"You can go now," he announced, gesturing me out of the sofa.

The next day he went to bed early again, claiming he didn't feel well. He sent my aunt to get me and she told me he wanted to talk with me. I went upstairs and sat on the floor beside his bed.

"I have to send you back to Portugal," he announced. "I cannot stand the thought of you going with someone who does not deserve you. If he comes after you there, then at least I won't know about it."

I felt as if my heart stopped in that moment, my world had been turned upside down. How could he do this?

"I don't know why you think so little of Paris when you don't know him." I offered, beginning to feel very emotional. "If it bothers you so much, I will end it with Paris, I just don't want to go back to Portugal. Please don't do that to me."

I was sobbing now, all the misery came back, I was back in my mother's house and was the saddest human being on this earth. I couldn't defend myself any longer, I just wanted to go back to my room and wait for the proverbial guillotine to end the life I had found and was building, in Canada.

"You say you would end it with Paris but if I found out you were seeing Paris secretly, it would kill me."

I calmed down my crying but the tears kept rolling down my face, my brain desperately trying to find a solution to this dilemma. I stood up and looked at him, lying on that bed, pale and seemingly in pain. "I don't want you to suffer on my account," I said. "If it means that much to you, I will end it all, I promise, you will never hear me mention Paris again. I do not want to be the cause of your suffering."

He seemed to calm a bit then said, "You are very young, Lourdes, study, find a job, then you'll see. You'll meet someone who deserves you and can take care of you. Now, stop crying."

"I never wanted to cause any trouble for you. I appreciate your bringing me to Canada and I am so sorry I unknowingly caused you to suffer."

He shook his head. "It's not your fault, it's just nerves but that's the way I am. Now, go to bed."

I said goodnight and went to my room. Sabrina was still awake when I got into bed but I didn't feel like talking. It saddened me to know I wouldn't be able to see Paris again but much more than that, I was upset to have caused my uncle such grief. Maybe he did care about me, maybe he was just as concerned as a real father would have been. When I finally ran out of tears, I fell asleep with my clothes on. In the morning I was still the unhappiest person in the universe.

In order to end it all with Paris I knew I would have to be cruel to him. But maybe if I were cruel, Paris would think differently of me. Maybe he'd think I wasn't worthy of him and I thought that might be easier for him. He called that evening not suspecting anything, and I told him I wanted to end the relationship.

There was silence on his end of the phone, then he seemed to gain control.

"Please take some time to think about it, Maria," he pleaded. "I love you."

"There is nothing to think about. I'm sorry, Paris," I said, then hung up.

I stayed in my bedroom for the rest of the night, wallowing in my misery. No one in the family bothered me, no one even called me to come down to dinner. Paris called several more times over the next few days, but I asked my cousins to tell him I wasn't in. Eventually he stopped calling and I felt a terrible loss. Maybe I was too young but it was so different to be with someone who wasn't after my body, someone who took pleasure in just being in my company.

Throughout my childhood and then again as a young teen in my mother's house, I had learned to live with sorrow. That ability had given me a certain inner strength that let me deal with just about anything that came my way. The misfortunes that befell me hurt—some deeper than others—but I was able to carry on. Disillusion and pain created a hard edge on me, strengthening my spirit. Over time I came to believe my life had been mapped out, that there were some roads I must avoid and others I must follow. Although the break-up with Paris seemed like another reverberating gong of unhappiness at the time, I convinced myself our relationship wasn't meant to be and carried on with my life, one step at a time.

I wish I had someone to confide in, a friend who would listen and advise me. I had Helen but she probably wouldn't understand, she was so gentle. But she was also wise, should I call her?

In the end I spoke with our friend, Arminda. She knew part of the situation and knew my aunt and uncle well. Always ready to offer encouragement, she convinced me it was time to find a job and get out of my relatives' house. Since she was well connected with the Portuguese community in Toronto, she thought she might be able to find me something temporary, at least until I was good enough with my English to go elsewhere. I assured her I would appreciate the effort and if she would refer me, I would try not to disappoint her.

A week later she called. She'd been listening to the Portuguese radio station and heard someone say they were looking for a girl between the ages of eighteen and twenty-three to work in a variety store in Toronto. I phoned the number she gave me and was told to come for an interview the next day. The little store was owned by a young Portuguese couple and they asked if I could start immediately. I smiled and assured them I would be happy to.

Going to my new job felt liberating. It felt as if I were at last on my way to becoming self-sufficient. On the first day, all I did was clean and stock shelves. The owner said that was the only way I would learn about the products they sold and at the end of the day, I agreed with him. I learned to operate the cash register the following day, and so began my working career in Canada.

The experience was new to me but I had always been thirsty for knowledge so I loved my job. Two weeks later I received my first paycheque and what a thrill. I went right to a bank and opened my very first account and the little book I was given showed I was the proud owner of account #56-50860, which boasted a balance of one hundred and fifty dollars. I had never had that much money in my life. I decided I could send at least twenty dollars to my mother but I would save the rest.

A couple of months later the owners of the store told me they trusted me to take care of their store by myself and that meant they wouldn't have to be there all the time.

Although I enjoyed working for these people who were very kind to me, most of our customers were Portuguese and after all the petty arguments with my family, I had vowed that when I had the means, I would live as far away from them as possible. I had also vowed never to marry a Portuguese man, since my experiences with them so far had brought me only heartache. I knew I was stereotyping, that not all Portuguese men were the same as the ones who had crossed my path up to that point, but the ones I'd known had left me bitter. Every one of them had been entirely self-righteous and demanding. I wanted nothing more to do with them.

I was satisfied with my job but the problems at home grew worse every day. My aunt rarely spoke to me and I considered leaving home so I wouldn't cause anymore grief. After all, I now had a job that paid enough that I could rent an apartment and live by myself. I spoke about the idea with my uncle and aunt because they were still responsible for me.

"I want you both to know how much I appreciate you caring for me for the past couple of years. I love you both and don't want to be the cause of any more concern. I have a job now and would like to release you of your responsibility. I am starting to look for an apartment so I can live on my own and be responsible for my own life. Thank you for everything, you'll never know how much I appreciate what you've done for me, but it's time for me to go."

I couldn't believe my eyes but after this long speech, they never said anything, they just exchanged a glance and went back to watching television.

I went away knowing no more than I had before the conversation.

That evening, my aunt came to my room and begged me to stay. "If you really want to go, feel free to do so, we won't stop you but I would like you to stay."

I had no idea what had prompted her sudden affection but she sounded sincere.

"Are you sure? It seems to me that since I arrived, all I have done is causing you grief. I don't want to do that, anymore."

"Hush, it's not your fault. Your uncle and I don't always see eye to eye and although we try to maintain the peace, things between me and him have been tense for a while."

"I'm sorry to hear that. Don't you think everything will be better if I'm not here?"

"No, the only people who can fix my marriage are your uncle and myself. It's nothing to do with you," my aunt finished with a sad note. "So please stay, save your money and when the time is right, then go on your own. But not now, you're not ready."

This conversation made me feel better and I knew I wanted to stay in this family, so I agreed.

A few weeks later, my uncle came home and announced that he had bought an apartment in Mississauga. They moved out of the rented house and I moved with them, but in spite of the new surroundings, our lives continued the same. My aunt, cousins and I, ate and played cards in the kitchen and my uncle was brought a tray with his food which he ate on his lap while watching television.

My salary at the variety store was only $75.00 a week so my savings were taking a bit to grow. I wanted to be on my own but I sadly realized that would not be possible for now. My determination became stronger when one day I noticed my uncle suddenly started looking at me differently whenever he talked with me. His expression was no longer that of a stern father figure, but one of such tenderness that it frightened me anytime I saw it on his face. I didn't think this new behaviour was appropriate at all.

After dinner one day when I picked up his tray to take it back to the kitchen, he lifted it up to me and whispered "Thank you," with a smile that I knew only too well—and so unacceptable and terrifying to me. I took the tray to the kitchen and then ran to the bathroom where I emptied my stomach of my dinner.

I went to my room after that and tried to understand my new situation. He was my uncle but I knew the look, it brought back echoes of what I went through with Mr. Santos. I had put that all behind me and tried to forget it but here I was, feeling confused and scared. Had I encouraged it?

No, never.

I was so lost and so desperate for a solution to this new situation but what to do? I had nothing and nowhere to go. There was not a person in the world who would care what happened to me. This man should be my protector, not my tormentor. When the pain was too much to bear, I dug a cave in my head and buried all the awfulness there, among all the other nastiness I didn't want to think about. The nightmares were about to resume.

I didn't get much sleep that night.

Chapter Fourteen

A Hard Bargain

After a restless night, I stood in the corner of the elevator holding onto my lunch bag, eyes downcast. Uncle stood beside me; his lunch box held by both hands in front of his knees.

My uncle drove me to the subway every day on my way to work. But on this day, he was unusually quiet. Not that he was the talkative type, but he didn't greet anyone when he came into the kitchen to pick up his lunch and that seemed odd. The children sat around the table eating their breakfast and my aunt was still in bed, tired from picking worms all night. I didn't care that he was silent, I just cared for this ride to the subway to be over so I could get on with my day. The elevator opened its door at the parking garage level and he got out first, leading the way to his car.

Once in the car he didn't move, didn't put the key in the ignition, just sat there, silent and staring like he was deep in thought. I waited, thinking perhaps he too had a sleepless night.

After a couple of minutes passed, I knew if we didn't leave soon, I would be late for work.

"What's wrong? Did you forget something?" I ventured.

He turned in his seat so he faced me and the sad look on his face began to worry me, I had never seen him look so...sad, so pathetic.

"Lourdes, I have been torturing myself for the past little while, not knowing what to do. I know this is wrong but I can't keep it inside me any longer. I love you."

What? What was he talking about and why was he telling me this?

I turned from him and focussed on my hands, resting on my lap. Suddenly the agony of understanding hit me. No, this could not be. Please God, I must've misunderstood him. The agony filled my chest.

"Please look at me," my uncle begged as he tried to touch the side of my face with the back of his hand. I slapped the hand away as if his fingers had burned my skin, my mind raced with unanswered questions.

Nightmares still assailed me every night and the images rose up before me.

The most frequent was of a man calling to me, his penis in his hand and a repulsive smile curving the corners of his evil mouth as he said my name.

In my other nightmare, I saw myself running for home. I reached the door but it wouldn't open. Suddenly it did and as I barely got inside, the man was there, trying to get at me. I couldn't close the door because he was stronger than me and when I screamed, the vision vanished and I woke up.

In my nightmares, I remained eleven years old, small and helpless.

"Please look at me," my uncle begged again.

I closed my eyes and prayed for all this to go away, for my uncle to come to his senses and to drive away from that underground that closed in on me, like a prison door. Maybe I should open the car door and run, but where would I go? I certainly could not go upstairs and tell my aunt. She would think it was all my fault, that I brought this on, or, even worse. She would buy a one-way ticket to Portugal and I would be back to my mother's house.

I sat in that car with my head down, tears streaming down my face as horrible helplessness filled every part of me. I felt his hand caress my head.

"I wish I wasn't in the situation I'm in," he said. "I know I'm much older and your uncle, I know this is crazy, but I've got to let you know what's in my heart."

All of a sudden, I felt a rush of heat rising from the very depths of me and I faced him.

"What are you talking about?" I slapped his hand away from me with disgust. "I can't believe what you're saying, it's just…so wrong. Why would I care what's going on in your heart? You're my uncle, for God's sake."

I covered my face and let out my misery. "Oh my God, my dear God," I whispered more to myself than to him. "I wish I was dead. I wish I never existed."

The key turning in the ignition all of a sudden made me look up at him. There was a wild look on his face that terrified me.

"Dead? You wish you were dead? Well so do I. Let's be dead together, this seems like a good day to die," he shouted and I covered my ears with both my hands. "If I can't have you, then I might as well be dead."

"No, please. NO.

He slammed the car in reverse. Terrified by his reaction, I grabbed his arm and the car went out of control, slamming against a pillar. He pulled into a vacant spot and said nothing at first, just sat and listened to me sobbing.

"Stop crying," he shouted with clenched teeth. "Don't you think I know how wrong this is? I didn't plan it, it just happened."

"You shouldn't let it happen, it's wrong. Very wrong." I shouted back.

He looked at me, his facial muscles relaxed now, a sad smile emerged as he held both my hands. "I suppose the only thing left for me to do is to put you on a plane and send you back to Portugal."

"You can't do that." I panicked. "Do you know what hell I lived through in my mother's care for the last ten years? Please don't do it, I'll do anything not to go back. Please." My uncle pulled me to him and kissed me on the lips, then he put the car in gear and drove me to the train station.

On the train to work, I couldn't help looking at everyone and wondering if any of the people around me had a heavy heart like mine. I wished I had someone to confide in, someone who would give me advice on what to do or give me shelter, so I could get away from the madness.

I went about that day in a haze. I was in a new country and could barely speak the language, I was without money or anyone who gave a damn.

But there was only one solution as far as I could see, put up with it until I could have a life of my own, but how? How could I tolerate my uncle's advances? How could I stand being intimate with someone I had once loved as if he were my father? It was all so disgusting, but what other choice did I have?

When I was a child and my aunt and uncle visited us in the village, my uncle had been the one to teach me how to tie my shoelaces and how to tell the right from the left of the shoes they had just brought me. I remembered all that.

By lunchtime, the scent of his cologne still lingered on my hands from his touch. Disgusted, I ran to the bathroom to rid myself of his smell, as well as everything in my stomach.

Acceptance of my fate came during the night, in my dreams. I knew what I had to do. I knew I had to survive this as I had survived my times with my mother and Mr. Santos, with acceptance and submissiveness. By morning I resolved to do the unthinkable in order to save my sanity…or lose it. My mind went into survival mode.

The next morning when I got into his car, I didn't fight him when he took me in his arms, I just closed my eyes so I wouldn't have to look at his face. I could pretend I was kissing someone else, and so I did but, in my heart, I despised this man as much as I had despised Mr. Santos.

From that day on I became my uncle's sex slave and I put up with that because I knew I would survive this, too. I will carry my disgust of him until my dying day. I will never forgive him for taking advantage of me in this way and betraying my trust.

I didn't know if it was apparent to the rest of the family but I winced every time he looked at me when we were all together. I don't know how he imagined that this relationship was going anywhere but the way he looked at me certainly told a story, I just hoped no one would notice it.

Little Sabrina adored me and her attitude towards me remained as loving as before. Roger and Pedro seemed distant and I couldn't help but sense their coldness and suspicion. My aunt too, behaved differently. She seemed jealous every time I played with little Sabrina and snapped at me at every opportunity. I had to interact with them and pretend everything was well in my world, and that was the hardest act I had to play.

One day, just shortly after my nineteenth birthday which was never celebrated, my uncle went shopping with his children. I was in my room and my aunt was still sleeping after working all night. When she woke up, she burst into my bedroom without knocking.

"How dare you, how dare you come into my house and steal my family from me?" She hissed accusingly, an angry look on her face.

"Auntie, what are you talking about? I would never hurt you and I don't want your family."

She looked like a wild woman and she was a lot stronger than me. I went around the bed to try and avoid her and then into the living room where there was more space. I hardly stepped into the living room before she grabbed my hair from behind. I immediately fell backwards while my aunt kicked me and pulled at my hair. I didn't defend myself. She came up with clumps of my hair in her clenched hands and I tried to fend off her blows. My cries came from the pain in my soul, for I knew I deserved this punishment.

My uncle and the children heard the commotion as they got off the elevator and stormed through the door. I was still down, my tear-stained face was battered and my hair strewn across the floor. The children held my aunt back and my uncle came to my aid.

"I am so sorry, this is all my fault," he said miserably. "Are you okay?"

I backed away from him, I did not want this man to touch me, ever again.

"Do I look okay to you?" I shouted. "Why don't you leave me alone? Why don't you all leave me alone?" I cried.

I ran to my room and didn't come out for the rest of the day or night and when Sabrina came in, I saw pity on her little face. I didn't sleep, though. All that was going through my head was a waking nightmare with the dreadful thought that I was going to be sent back to Portugal and to my mother. How was I going to prevent that?

By morning, I was so depressed I couldn't care less if I lived or died. When I heard screams coming from the living room I ran there and found my aunt kneeling over her husband's inert form, shaking him and trying to wake him. I ran to the phone and called 911. The ambulance arrived in a few minutes and after the medics examined my uncle, they said he was not dead but he had probably taken enough medication to put him into a coma.

"It's all your fault, you did this to him," my aunt shouted at me as she left with the medics to take her husband to the hospital.

My aunt came back later that day and told us that my uncle would have to stay in the hospital for a while under suicide watch. I kept to myself and stayed in my room out of everyone's way but found no light at the end of this dark and depressing tunnel. The next few days were tense for everyone but the children began to behave friendlier towards me again. I don't know how much they knew about me and their father but I certainly was not going to tell them. I would just have to bear my shame for eternity and that would be bad enough in itself.

The children and I sat in the kitchen a few days later when my aunt came in and sat next to me. "I'm sorry for hurting you," she apologized.

"Don't worry about it," I said, keeping my eyes down.

"He led me to it. This fighting would never have happened if he paid more attention to me," she continued, lips pursed. I looked closely at her then and saw that she looked regretful. I thanked God for this blessing. She couldn't have known what was really going on, otherwise I would be in the street by now.

"Do you know what he once did to your cousin, Pedro?"

"No," I replied, glancing at Pedro.

"Pedro has always been an adventurous boy," she explained. "He's always doing things just to see if he can get away with them and one day, he wasn't so lucky. I had gone shopping with the three children when Sabrina was just a baby. When we got home, I found Pedro eating a chocolate bar that I knew I had not bought for him and he didn't have money of his own," she said, pausing for effect as Pedro looked in my direction, abashed.

"After insisting that he tell me where he got it or he'd have to deal with his father, he finally told me that he put it in his pocket and forgot all about it."

I looked in Pedro's direction and he lowered his eyes.

"Thinking it would help Pedro learn his lesson so he'd never do it again..." My aunt's voice trembled as she raised both hands and rested them on her heart. "I told his father, never imagining that he would react the way he did. Imagine my shock when he got up from his chair, grabbed Pedro by the arm and dragged him into the kitchen. Once there and to my horror, he turned the stove on and when the element glowed red, he pressed Pedro's hand onto it." A tear slid down my aunt's face as she recalled the scene.

"The smell of my child's flesh burning was all over the house, I doubt it will ever be erased from my memory, or Pedro's.

We all fell silent. I was horrified by this.

A few days later my uncle returned home and nothing was ever said about his suicide attempt or what led to it. The household returned to some form of normalcy and my uncle never bothered me again. But the uncle/niece relationship would never be repaired.

No talk about sending me back to Portugal was ever uttered again, either.

Chapter Fifteen

New Beginnings

A few months into my job at the variety store, I noticed Eaton's department store was looking for a salesperson. Even though my English was much better than it had been, I still lacked confidence. I had no idea if they would even consider me but I was pleasantly surprised when I was granted an interview. On my interview day, I walked through one of the biggest chains in the country, imagining what it might be like to work there. I studied everything and everyone and silently asked God to help the Eaton's people like me.

After a detailed interview with the personnel manager, he said I was hired for a job in the Hostess shop. Shocked and thrilled at the same time, I started working there two weeks later.

I loved my first day at work and was so proud of myself. An exclusive grocery store and bakery combined; the Hostess shop offered customers imported grocery items not available in a regular supermarket. The most exotic teas, cookies, and spices tempted shoppers from the beautiful displays.

Of all the items we sold, two of them made an impact on me. Head cheese.

Why people would want to eat such greasy, horrible looking…whatever it was. It certainly didn't look anything like cheese, more like pork fat and other nasty stuff.

The other was Red Velvet Cake. It looked so delicious that I bought a whole cake shortly after I started there and took it home to share with the family. They loved it too. From then on, if I had to buy a cake, that's the one I got.

After working in the Hostess shop for a month, the manager told me that with my experience at the cash register, that's where I should work. Checking out customers wasn't difficult but I sometimes struggled to understand the people who phoned in, asking for things of which I had never heard. Even that stopped being an obstacle before long. Whenever I wasn't busy, I cleaned and rearranged the shelves to be familiar with everything we sold. It was like an adventure.

The sweet crooning floating from the record department next to the Hostess shop kept me in a good mood all day. I enjoyed my job but I soon began to think I would be happier if I were dealing with music instead of spices. One day, just a few months after starting with the store, I summoned up my courage and approached the record department's supervisor. A month later, I was working in the radio and music department where I learned all about different genres of music. I filled my mind with information provided by customers who asked me to look up a special song, artist, or composer. I especially enjoyed serving the older customers who often came in looking for old songs of which I had never heard. Some of these folks lived in a senior citizen's residence nearby and they often came in and stood in the aisle where a stereo system was set up, listening to the selected album of the day.

I also couldn't have asked for nicer people with whom to work. Right from the start, I made friends with two lovely co-workers: Ruth, my supervisor, was in her sixties, as was Violet, the woman who taught me everything I needed to know about the department. They were fountains of information and I listened closely to every bit of advice or knowledge they sent my way. I was a happy girl, I felt responsible and grown up. I still had moments when a new word would challenge me, but I would soon conquer it.

A year after I started working in the music department, Ruth retired. The manager, Mr. Vanderburg, asked me if I would consider supervising the department. I was shocked that he showed so much confidence in me after so little time but I told him I would love to. So, I became the new music department supervisor, where my job was to make sure my customers were happy and to make money for the store. At the end of each day, I went home smiling and thanking God for my many blessings.

While I was busy making sure my department was profitable, a young security officer had taken an interest in me. His name was Mac Lee and he worked at Eaton's part-time. He was very charming as he approached my counter and asked if I would go for a coffee with him. I smiled and accepted.

In the cafeteria, he seemed to want to make an impression on me by telling me all about himself. He was twenty-nine years old and originally from Trinidad, where his Chinese mother and Caucasian father still lived. His grandfather had apparently immigrated to Trinidad from Portugal but this young man looked nothing like the Portuguese men I knew. He wasn't cocky, he was somewhat shy and very respectful and gentle. He had dark hair, about five foot seven and walked with confidence. He seemed like a man who knew what he wanted and I had the feeling he wanted me. The day after we went for coffee, he brought me a red rose when he came in to work.

The romantic girl in me was very impressed.

A couple of days later, Mac invited me to dinner and after that, we saw quite a lot of each other. I liked him. He was charming and respectful and I didn't feel as if I had to pretend with him. I told him my story (excluding the nasty stuff) and he seemed to be comfortable with me. Actually, I thought he was going rather fast but at that time, I was still trying to get from under my relatives' control so I overlooked it. Getting special attention from a man who seemed to like me very much buoyed my spirits and my confidence.

A couple of months after I met Mac, I invited him to meet my family. They were polite, but they certainly didn't share our enthusiasm about our relationship. We weren't asked to stay for dinner or even just to sit down. We all stood in the living room while introductions were made. Sensing Mac's discomfort and my relatives' awkwardness, I told my uncle and aunt that we had to go. We were going out to dinner.

My co-workers, too, seemed reserved whenever Mac came around the department to see me. I noticed furtive looks in our direction when they thought I wasn't looking, but I wasn't going to let anything or anyone get in the way. I wanted to be with Mac and that's all that mattered to me. We had different backgrounds but what difference did that make? We were both young and could build a life together.

When I went home one day and told my uncle I was serious about this man, he tried hard to dissuade me from seeing him. He insisted the cultural differences were just too great and if I was looking for his blessing, I would never have it. I really didn't care for his blessing, I thought I should be considerate because I still lived in his house.

The next time Mac invited me to dinner, we had a good time as usual. He had so much to tell me about his family, the trip he had just taken to Trinidad and about his full-time job at a Revenue agency. When he finally drove me home at ten o'clock, my uncle was waiting for me in the lobby of our building. He looked as if he had not slept for days, so pale and gaunt he appeared. He looked at me accusingly, as if I had done something serious and wrong. He told me I had worried him because I didn't tell anyone I wasn't coming home after work. I kept silent while he went on to tell me that he didn't approve of Mac and this was really pushing it.

What had happened between us I had pushed into the deepest recesses of my mind so I wouldn't have to deal with it. I pretended all was the same as before that happened but obviously it was not working for him, he still wanted to have control over me.

I decided then and there that I would have to move out as soon as possible.

Up until that point, I had always depended on other people for my survival. First it was my grandparents and to them I owe a lot, if not my life. I often think of them still, though the memories make me sad. Only now can I see how little they actually had and appreciate how they never hesitated to share with me. My humble life with them made me feel happy and loved and I felt privileged to have known them.

Then I lived with my mother, the woman who always made me feel as if I was the most insignificant speck of humanity on this earth.

Finally, I had depended upon my aunt and uncle.

I calculated that with the savings I had and the salary I was being paid, I could probably manage food and rent. This realization sent me on a path of searching for an apartment. I hoped that someday I would be able to rebuild my relationship with my aunt but at that moment, I just wanted to break away and continue building a decent and solid future for myself. I would learn how to thrive with my new independence. There were no tears. I hugged my aunt, little Sabrina, Roger and Pedro and walked out of their lives, for now anyway.

I moved into a bachelor apartment on Niagara Street in downtown Toronto, and that was where I began to live my life as an independent woman.

The night I moved in, as I lay on my own sofa bed in that little apartment on the verge of sleep, my past hit me with the force of a cannonball, while my mind involuntarily recalled fragments of my former existence. There was no sobbing, just tears rolling down my face and onto my pillow. I was thankful for the small apartment that made me feel safe, and the opportunity to be on my own. When all the tears were spent, I fell asleep thanking God for bringing me this far in my journey and for all the lessons learned.

My aunt called me once in a while and I ended up visiting them at her request. My uncle remained cold and indifferent but as soon as I left their apartment, I forgot all the unpleasantness of being there.

I thrived in my job, I had a boyfriend who loved me and I led an independent life of my own. I was free to make decisions and, at almost twenty-one, I thought I was in the prime of my life.

Chapter Sixteen

A Young Girl's Dreams

On April 20, 1974, I celebrated my twenty-first birthday. Unlike in the past, there was no room for melancholy. I had the world in the palm of my hand. No longer the scared little girl with no shoes who was made fun of by the other children, I no longer got sent to bed without dinner. I had made something of myself.

I was at the front of the department rearranging records and getting ready to prepare a new display, when Violet tapped me on the shoulder. She said Mr. Vanderburg wanted to see me in his office. I was puzzled and a little concerned, but I didn't think I had done anything wrong. With a shrug I headed towards his office, followed by Violet.

As soon as I opened the door, many people yelled "Surprise!"

Violet caught me as I stumbled back, my heart racing. Everyone laughed and I looked around at all the people. Almost everyone I knew from the store was there, including some of the managers from other floors. When I asked, they explained that they had left skeleton staff on the floor so they could all be there. I had been on duty all day and never noticed anything going on. How had all those people managed to sneak into the office without my seeing them? Everyone gave me a present and Mr. Vanderburg handed me a huge card full of signatures. What a way to turn twenty-one.

The leadership and advice I received from Ruth served me well. The record department was successful and I wanted to keep it that way, but I also wanted to improve it if I could. I started paying attention to who came into the department and what they bought.

One day we received an album by a singer I hadn't heard of before by the name of Max Bygraves. He sang older popular songs such as "Me and My Shadow," "Yellow Rose of Texas," and "Moonlight and Roses" — songs that brought back memories to the older crowd. They came in almost daily and stood contentedly by the stereo system, listening to the whole album. Eventually, most of them bought one, and I smiled every time the cash register rang. Max proved to be such a success that soon I was ordering cases of his album. A few months later he recorded a second album, so I now had two with which to work. I played one in the morning and the other in the afternoon.

Unfortunately, listening to the same music every day, all day, annoyed the people who came for my birthday party. Some employees even complained to the store manager, since Mr. Vanderburg wouldn't listen to their complaints anymore. Why would he? The cash register in the record department never stopped ringing as long as those records kept playing. I don't think the employees got very far with their complaints because instead of being reprimanded, I received a raise. I now made the maximum pay in the supervisor's level salary.

Max released a third album, then a fourth. As a result, we had the highest sales in the history of the department. One day, Mr. Vanderburg told me Max was going to receive a gold record for the number of albums he'd sold, and the Royal York Hotel was going to host the presentation.

I was to be one of his guests of honour because he said I had been instrumental in making his music as successful as it was. At the party, I was delighted when Max approached me and thanked me for making this day possible. I loved him as soon as I shook his hand. He was friendly and personable, and because I had played his records for so long, I felt as if I knew him.

Sometime after Max's big night, a man came up to the counter where I was working and introduced himself as Glen Woods. Glen was the manager of men's wear and he wanted to know if I'd consider supervising his large department. The salary wasn't much better but though I loved working with music, I liked the idea of a new challenge, so I accepted.

Just over a year after we met, Mac invited me to dinner at Ports of Call, an impressive and popular restaurant in Toronto at the time. The eastern ambiance made it very exciting as I had never been in a restaurant like this one. I was fascinated when the waiter guided us to a low table with floor cushions to sit on.

I sat across from Mac and as usual, the conversation was all around our families and our jobs and getting to know each other better.

At the end of the meal, the waiter brought us fortune cookies and Mac raised his wineglass. "Let's drink a toast to this day, Maria, to our health and our future."

"Cheers," I said, raising my glass to his.

"These fortune cookies are very accurate, why don't you try one?" he said with a twinkle in his eyes.

"Sure they are. I've had fortune cookies before and they have not told me anything good. Are you saying these are different?"

"Try one, you may be surprised."

I smiled as he waited for me to take the small piece of paper embedded in it. I unfolded it and held my breath as I read the message on it. It said, *Maria, I love you. Will you marry me?*

Wow, I was surprised. I looked up at Mac and he was holding a small velvet box which he opened so I could see the diamond ring inside. He was smiling.

"Well, Maria, will you marry me?"

I was so happy at that moment. My dreams came true. I slid over to his side of the table and kissed him. "Yes, Mac, I will marry you." I said, glowing with happiness.

We went to visit my relatives that weekend to give them the good news. Their reaction did not surprise me. My uncle didn't bother to get up from his chair to congratulate us, he listened and when we finished talking, his gaze went back to the TV and I knew the meeting was over. My aunt gestured for me to follow her into the kitchen area and I did so, leaving Mac standing by the door.

"Are you sure you love Mac?"

"Of course, I do, very much," I responded. "He is attentive, polite and respectful. He never even suggested intimacy, even though he had plenty of opportunity to do so."

"Well, if you think this is what you want to do, I will respect that, but I just can't see you two together," my aunt replied.

I appreciated her honesty and as a show of appreciation, I gave her a hug which she returned. Walking back into the living room, I noticed Mac still standing by the door and my uncle still watching TV. "Uncle, I have no father, no one to walk me down the aisle. Would you please do that for me?" I asked.

"That's not a problem. I will," he said, not bothering to look at me or Mac.

I never let Mac know how much my relatives were against this marriage and I kept telling myself it didn't really matter if they approved or not. That's what I wanted and I envisioned myself married with children and a husband to care for.

We found a Catholic church and went to meet Father David who sent us to a marriage course in the parish. Mac's supervisor, Bob, was going to be our master of ceremonies and since he was involved with the church choir, he offered to sing at our wedding as well. Mac's cousin would be his best man and my little cousin Sabrina would be my flower girl. Since Helen, I never made friends with any other girls but I approached a girl in another department with whom I had talked with a few times. I asked her to be my maid of honour and when she got over the surprise, she agreed to do it.

I invited everyone I worked with because they were the only other friends I had. Mac's aunt and cousin came from Trinidad to attend our wedding as well

Chapter Seventeen

Tough Lessons

The day finally arrived when I became a bride. Like a princess in my wedding gown, I knew no one in the world could've spoiled that day for me. I went to my uncle and aunt's apartment the day before because I would go to the church from there. And in spite of not saying much, my uncle behaved like a gentleman when he gave me away. Bob sang *Ave Maria* instead of the traditional wedding march and the whole ceremony was a dream come true. We said our *I do*s and before I knew it, I was Mrs. Mac Lee.

We booked Ports of Call for our reception and that evening is a blur in my mind. On the other hand, my first night and following day as a married woman is quite vivid.

After the reception we drove four hours to Ottawa, to a motel

Mac had reserved for our honeymoon. We got out of the car and as I looked at the building, a feeling of dread invaded me. It looked old and not very welcoming. I looked around the parking lot to assure myself that no one was lurking around who could possibly do us harm. The area was not well lit but I didn't see anything suspicious going on. I noticed Mac looking around as well so I figured he didn't know what kind of a place he had booked at the time.

As Mac opened the door to our room and the light went on, the bed was the biggest thing in the room.

"Wow, that's quite a bed," Mac said as he walked over to it.

"Lots of room to play on," I said, looking around at everything in the room.

"Oh, look, it's a vibrating bed."

"What's a vibrating bed?" I walked over to where he stood.

"Sweetheart, you put coins in it and it will vibrate."

"Let's try it," I said, grinning.

Mac walked over to the bed to put some coins in the slot. I laughed as the bed started to shake as we laid beside each other. I couldn't stop laughing as the bed vibrated and Mac got caught up by my glee and started laughing as well. It only lasted for a few minutes and when the racket stopped, Mac turned to me, no longer laughing but with an adoring look on his face.

"You are so beautiful, sweetheart," he whispered, "I am such a lucky man." He then kissed me and when the temperature started to rise, I got up and told him I would get ready and be right back.

In the bathroom, I showered and then got out a silky, sexy negligee I had bought for this night. I wanted to be desirable to Mac and as I felt the material on my skin and looked in the mirror, I knew I was ready for my husband.

When I came out of the bathroom, Mac was already in the bed and looked at me with a look of approval on his face. He moved the cover aside and I got into bed with him. The kissing started and I so wanted to be with this man, I wanted to hold him and feel as if we were one, as if I would always be this happy. I wanted to explore and get to know my husband on a deeper level. I moved to shift positions and he moved as well, getting on top of me.

"Wait, don't rush it," I said with fervour. I wanted the passion, the foreplay. I didn't say this out loud and Mac continued with his ecstasy.

In a few seconds, it was over.

Desire left me, disappointed and frustrated.

"I'm sorry, sweetheart, I'll do better next time."

The following day we took the tour of the city and visited a museum where I learned a lot about Canadian culture. I wanted to know all there was about my new country and this was a great opportunity, but a mantle of apprehension had fallen over me about my new status.

After a lovely meal in a local restaurant, we went back to the motel room and the vibrating bed. We both didn't rush into bed but when we did, I was hoping this time it would be different, perhaps more romantic.

I didn't want the slam-bang-thank-you-ma'am, I wanted more. Even though it lasted a little longer, Mac apologized again and promised me it would get better.

I didn't believe him. "You know, I always thought my wedding night would be different," I said, more to myself than to him.

I didn't have any experience with marriage but I envisioned my first night with my husband to be magical, the happiest day and night of my life. It wasn't. I wanted so much to be happy, I thought I had found my Prince Charming when, in reality, Mac was someone who needed a wife as much as I thought I needed a husband. That evening, I knew the marriage was not going to work.

I didn't know what to do. Maybe it would change, I just had to wait and see.

But once doubt settled in my mind, I couldn't shake it. I had jumped from the hot frying pan right into the red-hot coals, without thinking of the long-term consequences. I longed for independence from my uncle and I chose my only option at the time. I went immediately from an imagined fairy tale relationship to the harsh reality of marriage.

Mac's aunt and cousin who came to the wedding never left to go back home, they settled with us in our two-bedroom apartment. At the time, Mac and I were still trying to understand married life. We stumbled along together and I kept hoping time would teach us to deal with our differences and save our marriage. We needed privacy and from day one we didn't have any. I understood that his culture was different than mine, that family was always welcome to live with you.

They were all very nice to me. Mac's aunt would cook and clean and once when she took a trip to China, she brought me back a pair of ruby earrings. I thanked her for the thoughtful gift and let her know that I appreciated the gesture. I liked her very much but her constant presence in my life didn't afford me any privacy with my husband. Most of the time I went to bed alone because Mac would always want to stay up with his family. So, our marriage continued to fail until it was clear that we were just a group of people sharing an apartment. A few months after we got married, his aunt's other daughter and a cousin came to study in Toronto so they too settled in with us. As they all interacted in their own dialect and obviously loved each other very much, I began to feel like a stranger amongst them.

A year passed and my dreams of a romantic union drained away. Every attempt I made to be intimate with my husband was repelled for fear of making noise or disturbing everyone. I had to stop keeping a marriage alive that died long ago.

On my twenty-third birthday and alone in my bed, I cried myself to sleep. The old melancholy came back and I had no idea what I would do with the rest of my life. I prayed to God for direction because I knew that only He could help me.

In contrast, everything at work was going well. When Eaton's announced that both their Toronto stores would be merging into what later became the Toronto Eaton Centre, I was offered a job at the new location as a supervisor for the small electronics department. Meanwhile, I knew I had to talk with Mac about our situation. I didn't feel as if I was married anymore.

The perfect opportunity presented itself one evening. We had been invited to dinner at Mac's supervisor's house, a one-hour drive from our apartment. Bob and his wife had always been pleasant to me so I managed to hide my feelings throughout the evening. Once we were on the highway heading back, I couldn't contain myself any longer.

"Mac," I began. "I want out of this marriage."

I looked at him for a reaction. I could see his knuckles turning white on the steering wheel but he didn't say a word. Then, he turned his signal on and made his way on to the shoulder of the road. When I looked at him again, I almost felt sorry for him but knew if I did, all this would have been for naught. So, I sat, determined to carry my mission to the bitter end. He pounded the steering wheel with frustration but I knew he must've been expecting this because when he finally found his voice, he said calmly, "Sweetheart, I know I haven't been the best husband to you and I'm sorry. Will you give me another chance?"

"I'm sorry too, Mac, I am sorry we both wasted precious time. Let's be serious, you don't love me and I don't love you, so let's stop pretending, shall we?"

"But, sweetheart, I love you." he replied vehemently.

"Maybe you did at one time or maybe you just took our marriage for granted, but I don't feel comfortable in it anymore. I want out, Mac, I can't make you happy and if we continue together, we're just going to end up hating each other."

"If I change, will you give me another chance?"

"No. If you change, it will be because you have to, not because you want to. I don't believe that would last very long. It's over, Mac, I'll be moving out this week.

A week later I moved in with a woman from work, Shirley, who had been looking for a roommate. Everyone stayed away from home the day I moved out. All I took with me were a few personal belongings and the furniture I bought for my first apartment. I never looked back. A month later a man came to see me in the store and gave me a manila envelope along with a small sentence. "This is for you. You're free."

I didn't leave my marriage with animosity or bad feelings, I simply thought it was not what Mac or I needed. I thought best to end it before any resentments started developing. Mac is a good man, a man who would have provided for our family if I had decided to go that route, but we were in no way compatible. I could only wish him the best in life and hope he found the love he was looking for.

Education had helped me before so I decided to take some courses in business administration. I signed up for an evening course at the Ryerson Polytechnical Institute in Toronto. The classes were somewhat boring, because anything to do with administration had to be recorded by hand in large, bulky ledgers. I easily passed the class.

Always thirsty for knowledge and wanting to learn about other related subjects, I enrolled in a Human Resources program being offered in the evenings at Seneca College. That course was easier because it was of more interest to me. I loved working with people.

For now, my job was satisfying but I wasn't having much fun. I always liked dancing, so I flipped through the yellow pages and found a jazz school. After a week of classes I discovered it didn't excite me, so I quit. I wanted to establish a regular exercise routine, though, so I enrolled in Tae Kwon Do classes. I stayed with that for over a year and managed to attain a green belt, but I eventually got bored with that, too.

Frustrated, I searched through the yellow pages again for something I might enjoy. That's when Jamile's Dancing Academy, a belly dancing school, grabbed my attention. The whole idea sounded mysterious and exciting. The first time I visited the school, I was met by one of the owners, Samira. In her lyrical middle Eastern accent, she explained that belly dancing had nothing to do with cabaret style dancing, as some people believed.

"It's an art form," she told me. "It is very erotic and sophisticated, yet graceful, dignified, and lovely to watch."

Samira led me to an ongoing class so I could see what it was all about. When we arrived, Samira's husband, Jamile, was putting the class through sit ups and similar exercises. A short time later I watched in awe as the students picked up veils and fluttered around the room, arms extended, veils floating behind them like the fluid wings of butterflies. I was enthralled by the music as well. The sounds of the Oud, a Middle Eastern stringed instrument, and the Tabla drum stirred something within me. I couldn't take my eyes away from a group of girls moving with grace, swirling and keeping time with the drum beats. I longed to dance so freely like them.

Compelled by the beauty of the dance, I signed up for classes and shortly after I received instructions on how to make my own belly dancing costume. I layered black silk fabric over a regular bra, then covered it with beads and sequins. I made a wide belt that rested on my hips, then set it over a flowing skirt made of many yards of silky black and silver fabric. My veil was made of the same silky material. It took me weeks to finish the costume but I was proud of it when it was completed.

After many lessons, Jamile choreographed a three-minute routine for me and I went to the school three to four times a week to practice it. I loved every step, every turn, every shimmy. Belly dancing allowed me to release all the negative energy that had built up in my body and soul over the years. I danced for me, for my joy, my ecstasy.

I also practiced with the school troupe, the "Desert Dancers". The group performed all over the city at venues such as the Canadian National Exhibition, the Japanese Cultural Centre, the Masonic temple, and in college auditoriums. In 1978, the school was asked to dance at a celebration of the fifth anniversary of the Scarborough

Town Centre. We danced inside the mall, performing group routines and our own personal solos. Hundreds of people crowded around and leaned over the second-floor railings. The area had to be roped off so there would be enough room for the dancers and television crews.

When it was time for my own solo routine, I was nervous at first, then I caught the eye of my roommate, Shirley, who had come to see the show. She pointed to the corners of her mouth, signalling me to smile, then the music carried me away. I danced, fluttered, shimmied, and smiled, but the smile wasn't for the crowd. The smile was for me.

One night, the school hosted an Open House. Several dances, including ballroom, were going to be demonstrated and a week before the event, Jamile asked if I would do the tango with him.

"You want me to do the tango?" I asked, astounded. "I have no clue how to do that."

"I'm your teacher, Maria, I will teach you the tango. You should have more faith, you're a beautiful dancer. Besides, we have a week to practice."

"A week to practice and then perform? Are you insane?"

He laughed. "I want you to learn the steps. Don't worry, I'll do the rest," he said, touching the tip of my nose.

Jamile was about five foot seven and had the typical middle eastern look. Dark hair and moustache and he had no trouble performing a belly dance routine, all turns and shimmies and the ability to charm his audience. He was a man of many talents. He was charming and his dancers were all female, so he possessed the art of manipulation. The idea of learning this intricate dance within a week seemed far above my capabilities but on the other hand, people kept telling me I was a good dancer so I decided to give it a try. With this kind of deadline, the pressure was on. I was at the school every day after work, practicing with my teacher. Learning the tango was more pleasant than I thought it would be and I found that once I learned the steps, Jamile's strong arms did the rest. I felt like a marionette, spinning and flying on command.

Saturday arrived and I took special care with my dress, a knee length, royal blue chiffon creation. My long hair was carefully piled into a chignon, with curled ringlets cascading down my back. My shoes matched my dress and when I looked in the mirror, I smiled at my appearance. I liked what I saw.

The ballroom was filled to capacity. People sat on chairs around the outer edge and more stood behind them. Samira was the emcee for the evening and when she introduced us as the couple demonstrating the tango, I thought my heart would jump right out of my chest.

While I was waiting backstage, a glass of Chivas Regal magically appeared in Jamile's hand. He held it in front of my mouth.

"Drink it," he said.

"What?" I frowned, confused. "Not only do you want me to do a dance I'm not familiar with, now you want me to do it while I'm drunk?"

He snorted and shook his head. "It's just an ounce. It'll get rid of the butterflies. Drink up."

I downed the liquid and the moment I was done, he grabbed my hand and guided me to the dance floor.

"Smile," he said between his teeth.

Once onstage, we stood ready, waiting for the music to start. My back was as straight as a ballerina's, one of my hands in his, and the other rested on his shoulder. He'd planted his other hand firmly on my lower back and his encouraging smile was infectious. I soon forgot all about being nervous. He either spun my whole body or made my head turn this way or that with a mere twist or press of his hand on my waist. All I could do was keep smiling and following his lead. Before I knew it, we were bowing and the crowd was applauding. It was an incredible experience. Jamile was not only a great instructor, the man was a phenomenal dancer, and so was I.

Because belly dancing was popular at that time, the school was asked to host a show for the French television channel. I was invited to participate in the televised demonstration and when I looked at the video later, I was pleased with what I saw. The shy belly dancer who had once performed at the Scarborough Town Centre was gone. On my TV screen I saw a beautiful and proud young woman, not afraid to show her smile. I was in the best physical shape I had ever been; this new self-esteem and confidence were opening the door to a life I had only dreamed about. Belly dancing had definitely been a step in the right direction.

I felt my life begin

Chapter Eighteen

Friends Conspire

I continued taking lessons at the school and participating in demonstrations. Now, as one of the senior dancers, I was often asked to take over a class.

One night, one of my troupe mates, Carol, approached me.

"Maria, the German Cultural Club is looking for a belly dancer for their annual ball. Would you consider dancing for them?"

"You're a good belly dancer, Carol. Why don't you do it?"

She smiled and shrugged her shoulders. "I really don't want to dance for my friends," she admitted.

I gladly accepted the challenge.

I have never since been to anything that could compare to a German ball. I went to the club on the date I was given and waited in the dressing room until dinner was over. Then I was introduced. My music, a smooth flute melody right out of Arabian Nights, filtered through the speaker system, loud and clear. The lights were dimmed and all I could see were shadows around the large dance floor. The music filled my senses. I glided into the room, soft steps, fluttering veil and skirts, the scent of Eternity filling the air around me. I was totally lost in my performance.

When the tempo changed to a livelier beat and I could clearly hear the Tabla, the lights were turned on again. They later told me that I appeared out of control. I danced and smiled while I did it and the applause from my audience gave me confidence, filling me with energy. On the very last beat I bent my knees and dropped backwards to the floor. There was a hush in the crowd as they wondered if I was all right. I expected this and after a couple of seconds, my arms crossed at the wrists while my twirling hands stretched and reached up, my heart beating wildly from the long drum solo. The audience broke into applause again after realizing that dropping suddenly to the floor was part of the routine. I rose gracefully, bowed to everyone and left the room.

Back in the change room, I slipped into evening attire then joined the club's entertainment director, his family and friends at their table, as he had requested. Compliments poured out of everyone and as I looked around the room, smiles beamed at me from every direction. Even the club's Prince and Princess, sitting at the head table, looked at me and smiled. I was thrilled.

Later on, the happy melody "Roll Out the Barrel" sounded from the adjacent room and dancing girls marched in, followed by a six-man band that played all evening. Women in long flowing gowns were swept across the floor by tuxedo-clad men. Charming, cultured and friendly, these people made me feel as welcome as an old friend, even though we had just met.

While all this excitement in my life was going on, I was still working at Eaton's, but the routine at work left me restless. I wanted to explore other fields and after doing some research, banking seemed like a good idea. Fortunately, I had no trouble attaining a job as a teller at Victoria and Grey Trust on Bay Street, in Toronto's financial district. I was sad to leave all my friends at Eaton's, but the prospect of a new job and new adventures made it all very exciting. By the time I turned twenty-seven I no longer lived with Shirley, I had my own apartment and was the proud owner of a small Toyota. Once again, my wages didn't stretch far enough to cover all my living expenses, especially after the purchase of a car, so I supplemented my income by occasionally working as a waitress in the evenings. There was little else I could pack into my days without total exhaustion.

I still didn't have many friends outside my work or dance circles but one day, I was in one of the practice halls working on a new routine when I noticed a tall woman standing in the hallway, watching me.

She peeked through the open the door. "Do you mind if I come in?"

I hesitated for a moment. I had not seen many women as tall as her but her friendly smile put me at ease. "No, of course not, come on in." I replied, heading towards the door to welcome her.

"My name is Lola and I'm also a student here," she said, extending her hand.

I took it, smiling up at her. "Hi, I'm Maria, I don't think I have seen you before." I couldn't imagine not noticing her nearly six-foot frame before but Jamile had many students and classes. "How long have you been belly dancing, Lola?"

"Longer that I care to admit. Unfortunately, I have an aggressive type of arthritis and I have to keep moving. When I was fourteen, my family physician told me that I would probably be in a wheelchair by the time I was 30. Well, so far so good. I have been practicing this art since I was eighteen, so that would make it ten years. How about you?"

"Not as long as you, I'm afraid. You must be really good at it."

"Well, don't know about being good, but I listen and try to learn as much as I can. I was watching you from the doorway. You have a lot of potential. Do you mind if I give you a few pointers?"

I didn't hesitate or stop the grin that landed on my face. "I'd love it, thanks."

So, Lola and I practiced together and my dancing improved. From then on, I tried to come into the Academy when Lola did and soon, we became fast friends. One evening, she invited me to go out to dinner at a restaurant featuring belly dancing. I had never seen belly dancers from other schools, so I was curious and excited to go.

Dinner and conversation were very good and when the show started, we both noticed that the dancers had been taught a very different and more exotic style of dance than our own. One of the girls, Robyn, came to our table to say hello after her show, and Lola and I invited her to sit with us and have a drink. She was friendly, pretty and outgoing.

I couldn't contain my admiration. "I've got to tell you, Robyn, I loved your routine. A bit different than the dancing Lola and I do but beautiful just the same."

"Different? In what way?" Robyn asked.

"I see your dance more of a Cabaret style dancing, while ours is more traditional," Lola volunteered.

Robyn smiled and nodded. "*Hmm*, I see. I would love to see your style, sounds interesting."

"Where do you live?" I asked.

"I live in Newmarket and work in Scarborough."

"Newmarket's not too far from my place," I said. "Hey, Lola and I practice in my apartment on Weston and the 401 on Saturdays, would you like to join us? That way you could see our dance and we could see yours. Does that sound good?"

"I'd love that, sounds wonderful. What can I bring?

"How about a bottle of Spumante Bambino? If you decide to join us every Saturday, we can celebrate." I couldn't contain my enthusiasm.

"Done, I'll see you both on Saturday," Robyn said after I gave her my address.

Saturday arrived and so did Lola and Robyn. We had coffee and talked a bit about our dance.

Robyn had lots of questions. "So, tell me, where have you danced? Do you dance as a group, or solo?"

"Both," Lola offered. "Most of the time we begin the show with a group routine followed by some solos. Why don't you show us some of what you do and we will do the same?"

Robyn put some music on and Lola and I sat and watched. Suddenly Lola gets off the couch and lays on the floor looking up at Robyn.

"Hello up there," she waves. "We're both sitting on the sofa, Robyn. Why are you looking at the floor when you dance?"

"I get it, thank you."

We all laughed.

We had such good times. It was from those days that another lifetime friendship was formed, one that lasted long after belly dancing had been forgotten. Lola eventually faded from my life but Robyn became to me the sort of friend who would stand for my soul.

Life continued to be good. I was asked to dance at the German club anytime they had anything to celebrate and, through them, I met a couple from Newmarket, a small town just north of Toronto.

Elizabeth Lacasse was a solidly built and friendly German/Canadian woman in her early fifties. She was also assertive and knew exactly what she wanted. Her attitude was plainly "Don't mess with me" and "Listen to what I have to tell you because it's for your own good." Her husband George was ten years younger than his wife and he enjoyed working at the exotic car dealership they owned.

Once they got to know me and knew I was on my own, they invited me to their home some weekends. I felt as if I had a family as well, since I didn't keep in touch with my own very often. If I didn't have to work on the weekend, George would pick me up at my apartment on Friday—sometimes in a shiny new Porsche. I refrained from smiling all the way up Highway 404, as other motorists looked in our direction with admiration. And maybe just a little envy.

George and Elizabeth Lacasse didn't have any children and I never saw any relatives visiting, so after a while it became like I was visiting my parents or dear relatives. Once in a while some friends from the German Club would visit but that didn't happen very often. One Saturday when I was visiting with them, Elizabeth announced that she had invited some friends to join us for dinner that evening.

"Danny Trautman has been our friend and business associate for many years," she said.

"I'm sure it'll be nice to meet him," I responded.

"Oh, you've already met him, Maria. He and his girlfriend Kelly came to visit when you were here, some time ago."

I tried to recall a face. "I don't really remember meeting either of them, Elizabeth."

"Oh, you'll like Danny, Maria," she said with a conspiring look

"Well, if they're friends of you and George, I'm sure I will like him."

When the doorbell rang at five o'clock that afternoon, I answered it. There stood a handsome and smiling man in his thirties, surrounded by three young girls.

"Hello there, I'm Dan, and who are you?" I couldn't help but smile back, shaking his hand in greeting.

"Hi," I said. "My name is Maria and I'm a friend of the Lacasses. Come on in, Elizabeth will be with you shortly."

"Thank you," he said. "You may not remember me, Maria, but I think we met at one of your previous visits." His smile was warm.

I must have looked a little befuddled as I tried again to think when I had met him. Surely, I would remember him.

They stepped into the hall and before anyone had the chance to say another word, the youngest girl grabbed my hand and shook it vigorously, introducing herself. "Hi, I'm Claire."

Her father laughed. "Well, you'd better meet the others," he said, and introduced Louisa, his eldest who smiled politely at me, and Shelby, who looked at me coolly then walked past without saying a word. Elizabeth bustled out of the kitchen, smiling and drying her hands on a tea towel. She greeted all of them and then ushered everyone to the living room. George was in his favourite chair, relaxing and watching the ball game. He got up, shook Dan's hand and hugged all the girls.

"Danny, you sit and talk with George," Elizabeth said, "and maybe the girls would like to help Maria set the table."

Claire immediately put her hand up. "I will, I will."

She followed me into the dining room and didn't stop talking the whole time we were setting the table. She wanted to know everything about me and by the time we re-joined Elizabeth in the kitchen, I knew everything about her family as well.

"My parents are divorced," she informed me. "Dad used to go out with Kelly but they got mad at each other one day and we never saw her again. She was his girlfriend, you know. He doesn't have a girlfriend now."

"How old are you, Claire?" I asked.

"I'm almost ten. My sister Shelby is twelve, and Louisa is the oldest. She's fifteen."

"Do you live with your dad?"

"No, we live with my mom but we visit Daddy every weekend. Dad's too busy," she said, frowning with disappointment. "He's an electrician and he's always working."

I studied her sweet face and wondered how this child could be so friendly and outgoing, considering she just met me. I couldn't help but be drawn to her innocence and honesty.

I listened to her chit chat and when we finished setting the table, she took my hand and led me back to the kitchen.

"I see you made a friend," Elizabeth said. She handed me a big platter to set on the table.

I smiled as I turned to leave the room again. "Yes, I did, Claire and I were just getting acquainted."

"Where do you live?" Claire asked, still on my heels. "I've never seen you before."

"I live in Toronto."

"Toronto? Really? I was in Toronto once, when Kelly and Dad were still together. We went to the Exhibition."

"That's one of my favourite places to visit, Claire."

"Mine too. I wish we could go back," she said, her eyes wide. "I loved all the rides, especially the roller coaster. I liked the food pavilion, too, it was fun trying all the different foods."

By the time everyone was finally seated for dinner, Claire and I were buddies.

Elizabeth liked to talk and sometimes would dominate the conversation. Although nothing was different that evening in that respect, I suspected this gathering hadn't happened by accident.

"Thank you for helping Maria, Claire, I heard you chatting away in there. Did you find the two of you have a lot in common?" Elizabeth asked, smiling kindly.

"We both like Toronto and the Exhibition," I replied, winking at Claire.

"Ah, I remember the Exhibition, I remember that place from when we were younger and not so busy, *neh*? George?"

"Oh yes, my dear, I remember it well," George answered, interrupting the conversation he was having with Dan. "That place is for young people, you wouldn't see me going on any of those rides."

Elizabeth then turned to Shelby.

"And you, Shelby, how's school?"

"Good." The girl said without looking up. She continued picking at her food as if the Lacasse house was the last place in the world she would have chosen to visit. Elizabeth took the hint and left her alone.

"Louisa, here you are, a pretty young lady," Elizabeth continued. "It seems like only yesterday when all you girls would come and visit and all of you would run around the yard, chasing my little puppy Bebe. That must mean I'm getting to be an old woman, I suppose." She smiled at the children and turned to me. "Danny is an electrician and runs a very successful company here in Newmarket." She shifted her attention back to him. "How's business, Danny?"

"Quite good, Elizabeth, got all the guys working and I'm also working hard, trying to earn a living as usual," he responded casually as he helped Claire cut the meat on her plate.

"You work too hard, always did." She looked at me to make sure I was paying attention to the conversation but I had nothing to contribute so I just smiled and kept silent.

"But you know, Danny, too much work and not enough play makes for a dull life. You've got to have some fun."

The conspicuous glint in Elizabeth's eyes confirmed my friend was on a mission.

"The same with Maria, this girl works too much and that's why we try to get her out of the city once in a while, when she is not working weekends as well. Not that we are fun company but at least she is not alone in that little apartment."

I glanced across the table at Dan and I suspected he was also appraising the conversation. I found him very interesting, I had never met anyone like him. All the city boys who ever showed any interest in me did not compare to this clean-cut-looking but rugged and obviously tender and caring man. His height, which I guessed to be about six feet two and his rugged lumberjack look, made him appear sexy and appealing. I couldn't deny the attraction but he had a family and a girlfriend who may come back to him, so why would he even consider me? Nah, better just enjoy the meal and the company and stop having romantic notions in my head.

"Who's up for ice cream?" George asked standing up, his eyes wide and smiling at the girls.

Claire didn't need any prodding, she immediately got up and followed George into the kitchen.

After dinner, Elizabeth and I cleaned up the kitchen and little Claire volunteered to help. She was vivacious and full of curiosity and she chatted freely with Elizabeth. Once in a while she'd look at me and smile as if she held the most precious of secrets. When the clean-up was done the three of us returned to the living room where the other two girls watched TV and the men enjoyed a glass of brandy.

Dan was courteous and charming. His daughter Louisa was polite but reserved. I looked at Shelby at one time and from the expression on her face when she looked back at me, I thought for sure something rude would explode from her lips. Perhaps she was perceptive enough to realize as I already had, that this evening was one of Elizabeth's master plans.

It was almost ten in the evening when Dan announced it was time to go home. Everyone got up to say their goodbyes and Dan took my hand in his, his hand was warm and welcoming. It enfolded my smaller one and the squeeze was like a whole-body hug, friendly, intimate and all-around delicious. The warm energy of his hand enveloped my whole body and mind. I had shaken many people's hands in my lifetime and I had just met this man, but…I would never forget that moment or that handshake.

"It was a pleasure seeing you again, Maria," he said looking right into my eyes.

"Likewise," I managed, a little flushed.

Louisa nodded and said goodnight, Claire threw her little arms around my neck and kissed my face, and Shelby left without even looking in my direction. That meant little to me, as I thought I probably would never see them again.

When I went to bed that night, my thoughts revisited the evening and rested on Dan and his children. What happened between Dan and his girlfriend, Kelly? He seemed like a wonderful man and I had trouble imagining anyone wanting to leave him. Or, maybe he left her.

These thoughts rolled around in my head for a while and continued to resurface as I tried to sleep. Finally, I decided there was nothing to be gained by thinking about it any further and it was none of my business.

The following week, Elizabeth called me at work and asked if I would come to Newmarket for the weekend. I readily agreed. After lunch on Saturday, she wanted me to go shopping with her and it wasn't until she stopped at a house in a part of town far from the shopping district that I realized my friend had no plans to go shopping at all.

"This is Danny's house, Maria," Elizabeth said matter of fact as she got out of the car.

"Why are we at Dan's house?" I asked wide-eyed and panicky.

"Well, I thought since we were in the area, we could stop and at least say hello."

The expression on her face clearly told me she was in total control of the situation and there was no going back. I was not only surprised, I was embarrassed. What would the man think? I had just met him. On the other hand, I knew that if I refused to go to the door with her, Elizabeth would make a scene which would be much worse. Dan would hear us and come outside and think this was all my idea. Oh my God, what to do? I wish there was a big rock nearby where I could hide but, by this time, Elizabeth was already ringing the doorbell.

When Dan came to the door and realized it was us, his smile somehow made me feel even worse about intruding on his privacy. I felt very, very awkward. I had to remind myself that Newmarket was a small town and perhaps people did this all the time, visiting without giving notice. Then too, this was Elizabeth, she was audacious and relentless when she wanted something and undaunted by convention.

Dan stood there, smiling, in his track pants and t shirt—still looking handsome in my eyes. And my eyes didn't want to look at the welcoming smile on his face because I was just too embarrassed, standing there in the driveway while Elizabeth was gesturing for me to come inside and visit.

Dan's children sat on the floor around the coffee table, eating pizza. My stomach tightened from embarrassment for interrupting his meal with his children.

" Hello, everyone," I said, and then almost bolted when I looked at Shelby. The look on her face clearly said, "What the hell are you doing here?"

Really? What did I ever do to this person?

"Would you ladies like to join us for some pizza?" Dan politely offered gesturing for us to come and sit on the sofa.

"No, thank you," I managed.

"That's okay, Danny, you enjoy your lunch with your children. I was just showing Maria our town when we passed your house and I had to stop and say hello, *neh*? Maria?"

"Sure, of course. It was nice seeing all of you again," I said, directing my words at Dan as I turned to leave.

"Well if I can't talk you into having some pizza, how about a glass of wine?"

The triumphant smile on Elizabeth's face told me I was doomed to stay. "Yes please, Danny, that would be lovely." And she sat down while Dan walked into the kitchen to fetch the wine.

"White or red?" Dan asked from the kitchen.

"Red for me, please—how about you, Maria?"

"Red is fine, thank you," I acquiesced.

Louisa and Claire had stopped eating but Shelby continued munching on her pizza, not paying attention or perhaps paying very much attention to what was going on.

Louisa smiled at me when I looked at her and little Claire patted the sofa beside her.

"Will you sit beside me, Maria? It's nice to see you again," she smiled innocently.

A few moments later Dan came back with a bottle of red wine and three glasses, smiling as if this was the most natural thing in the world. As we sipped our wine, Elizabeth made small talk while Dan and I listened and made appropriate comments. Suddenly, one of the girls squealed and all three jumped to their feet. Red wine landed on the carpet.

"Don't panic," I said standing up. I turned to Dan. "Do you have any white wine?

Dan gave me a quizzical look but then rushed into the kitchen and came right back with an open bottle of white and a rag. By the looks on all their faces, I knew they were all wondering what I was up to. I kept my voice calm. "You see, white wine has an enzyme that neutralizes the stain caused by the red wine. It makes it easier to clean."

I got down on my knees with the wine-soaked rag to erase the spreading stain and to my relief, it was working.

Without any warning, the rag was snatched from my hand by Shelby who knelt down beside me and started scrubbing at the carpet. "I'll do that," she hissed; her tone stiff with superiority.

"Don't scrub, Shelby, blot," I said.

A few minutes later and to my relief, Elizabeth stood up and took Dan's hand. "Well, we must go and let you enjoy the rest of your lunch. It was nice to see you, please come visit more often. Bye girls." She smiled and waved goodbye.

"Thank you for the wine," I said, happy to be going.

Back in the car, I kept silent even though I wanted to tell Elizabeth that was a very bad idea. What did Dan think? Did he think it was my idea? Oh God, I hoped not.

Elizabeth glanced over at me and smiled. "Well, Maria, what did you think of Danny's house? Nice, eh?"

"Very nice," I responded sounding disinterested.

***

George and Elizabeth's car dealership handled only the most exotic cars, so their clientele was the crème de la crème of Toronto.

In 1983, they decided to add a more economic car to their line-up. I was thirty years old when the Hyundai Pony made its entrance into Canada. Their dealership held a party to celebrate the event and Elizabeth asked me to be the hostess. I felt honoured and even agreed to wear a snug-fitting Japanese style dress. With my long dark hair, I was dressed for the part. The photographer hired for the day took pictures of me and the Pony, sitting inside of it, standing beside it, and just about draped over the car. We were the stars of the show.

When the last of the guests departed, I proceeded to meet Elizabeth in her office and was surprised to see Dan there.

"Hello again, Maria," he managed to smile, but I sensed he wasn't feeling well by the tired look on his face. He stood as I came into the office.

"Elizabeth asked me to come and host the party with you," he said, "but I came down with this awful cold a few days ago and I couldn't shake it."

"I'm sorry to hear that, Dan. Don't worry about it, the presentation went well," I said with an encouraging smile.

Elizabeth had stood listening to our exchange, waiting for an opportunity to have her say. "Well, now that you're here, I hope you can join us for dinner, Danny," she put in.

"I'm sorry to disappoint you, my friend," he said, "but the only reason I'm here is because I promised you that I'd come."

"And we're happy to see you, aren't we, Maria? And you still have to eat, right?"

I wished for another rock to hide under. Why was she putting me in the middle of this? I wished she would just let the man go home.

"I can't, really," Dan said, "As you can see, I'm still wearing my work clothes."

That was not going to deter Elizabeth. "Maria," she started, turning to me. "You don't mind if Danny comes to dinner with us in his work clothes, do you?"

I wanted to say "Yes, I do," so Dan could go home and rest, but I didn't want to appear rude or make him think I didn't want him there. "No, I don't mind your work clothes," I said with a reassuring look.

"It's settled then, I'll go and get George and we'll go to dinner."

"Okay, I guess there is no sense arguing with you, my friend," he shrugged his shoulders and smiled.

At the restaurant, I ordered a seafood pasta dish I had enjoyed there previously and when Dan said to the waiter, "I'll have the same as Maria," the sound of my name on his lips in this context gave me a little tingle.

The talk during dinner was all about cars and how the open house had turned out and when all the goodbyes were said and done, I was sad to see Dan go. I hoped our paths would cross again and when I went to sleep that night, visions of him filled my thoughts.

Chapter Nineteen

Romance

A couple of weeks passed since the presentation of the Pony and during that time, I found my thoughts often going to Dan. When Elizabeth phoned and wanted me to go shopping with her, I agreed. It was always an adventure to go shopping with my friend. Her enthusiasm was contagious and at times I felt almost as sophisticated as she, even though I could never afford to buy anything for myself. She asked me to meet her at one of her favourite boutiques, a few blocks from the dealership. As the salesclerk packed up the most amazing clothes like silk blouses and leather skirts and such, Elizabeth turned to me. "Come to dinner with me and George, Maria."

"Thank you but I don't think so, I have had a busy day and am tired, I just want to go home."

"You must come, *neh*? We love your company."

It was always difficult for me to say no to Elizabeth. I was heading towards my parked car when she suddenly grabbed my arm and said, "Come with me, Maria, leave your car here and we'll get it afterwards."

"You want me to leave my car in this parking lot? Wouldn't it make more sense to leave it at the dealership where I know it'll be safe?" I asked, puzzled.

"Oh, stop fussing and come with me. Your car will be safe here."

I didn't get it. She took hold of my arm and led me to her car and I followed, reluctant. I began to doubt her sanity but when we got to the shop, it all made sense. She wasn't insane, this was part of her mission.

George and Dan sat in the office when we walked in and I thought the look on Dan's face must've mirrored my own. I was embarrassed by the obvious set-up but secretly pleased at the same time. From the expression on his face, Dan didn't know I was going to be there, either.

"Hi, Danny, it's so good to see you," Elizabeth gushed, going over and giving him a hug. "I talked Maria into going to dinner with us, isn't that great?"

When she released him, Dan came over and said with a smile, "It's so good to see you again, Maria," he winked at me and that made me feel better. He knew we were being set up.

The Lacasses did everything in style. One of their favourite things was to eat in the best restaurants, the sort of places the hungry wouldn't go because in spite of the large plates, it wasn't quantity, but rather, the presentation that mattered.

Dinner as usual was fabulous. The rack of lamb was cooked to perfection and the roasted potatoes and veggies had some kind of delicious sauce dribbled on them. Dinner looked like a work of art.

The evening was pleasant and made even better by the fact that we were seated at a small table and I could feel the warmth of Dan's body next to mine.

At the end of the evening, it was clear why Elizabeth wanted me to leave my car parked outside that little boutique.

"Danny," she asked sweetly, "would you mind driving Maria back to her car?"

He smiled. "I don't mind at all; it will be my pleasure."

"I'm sorry you have to go out of your way," I said to Dan as I climbed into his Yukon, "It appears Elizabeth is determined to be a matchmaker."

"You noticed that as well? I have known what she's up to from the time we had dinner at her house. She is a determined woman. How do you feel about what she's doing?"

"Just so you know, I had nothing to do with it and I have not encouraged her in any way. But you're right, she is strong-willed." I ventured a look at him and we both smiled.

Elizabeth, that crafty woman, had made sure that my car was parked far enough so we would have the chance to talk and get to know each other better. When we arrived at the little parking lot, we were just getting started.

"Do you want to get a cup of coffee, Maria? I know a little deli just down the road."

"That would be great, let's go."

By now we behaved like old friends. I felt at ease with Dan and had no qualms about opening up to him.

I told him about my failed marriage, my job, my involvement with the German club, and the story I had told everyone else including George and Elizabeth. I was born in Portugal, raised by my grandparents and later lived with my mother who was not a very nice human being. I came to Canada at the request of my aunt when I was almost eighteen and I was now living on my own.

It was a nice and clean story.

"Well, as you know by now, I recently broke up with my girlfriend, and I suspect that's why Elizabeth wants us to be together.

"You may be right," I said with a nod.

"I loved that woman," Dan continued, "but she decided that my best friend was a better match for her. I was heartbroken but I cannot tell her what to do. I'm a fisherman and a hunter when time allows me and I stay away from home for days at a time. I feel that's why she left me."

He had a sad but resigned look on his face and just then, I wanted to hug him.

"You know what they say," I tried to cheer him. "If you love someone, set them free. If they come back after leaving you, shoot them down."

We both laughed.

"I don't think that's the way it goes, is it? he asked, grinning.

"No, not really."

"I feel good in your company, Maria, You're a good listener. Thank you for that," he said after a few cups of coffee.

"That's the least I could do, after dumping my whole life story on you," I said.

He drove me back to my car and while still holding the door he said, "You're a very nice person and I like you, Maria. When I get my head straightened around, would you go out to dinner with me? Alone?"

"I would love to," I said, returning his smile while he held my hand. "Call me when you're ready."

Dan closed the car door and I drove away, pleased that we had established a promising connection. I hoped I had eased his pain by being his friend and listening to his story. I got the impression that maybe he had decided that what happened between him and Kelly had been for the best.

When I got home, my heart was full of his gentleness, his sincerity and the peace of how comfortable we felt in each other's company. Now that I'd come to know him better, I realized he was the type of man I had been searching for all my life. I couldn't wait to see him again.

A month passed and I had not heard from Dan. I was disappointed and wondered if perhaps he made up with Kelly and forgotten me. Through our conversation the last time we met I could see that the man was still in love—it showed in the sadness on his face whenever Kelly's name was mentioned. I tried to distract myself but I couldn't get him out of my head. The more I thought about him the more I missed him and the knot in my soul tightened.

For the first time in a long time, I felt sad and alone. Had I fallen in love? Was Dan the right man for me? I didn't want to admit these things to myself but every thought of Dan left a rush of anxiety in my chest, a clinging sadness at the possibility that I might never see him again.

Each night I went through this agony and each night I tried to convince myself that I could not control destiny. If Dan was meant to be mine, then God would bring him back to me.

One bitter cold January morning, the phone rang.

"How are you, Maria?"

My heart warmed at the sound of Dan's voice. "I'm fine, how are you?"

"Good to hear, I'm fine too, thanks for asking. I was wondering if you would like to go to dinner with me sometime."

For a moment I couldn't breathe. Then I answered, "I would love to, when?"

"What about Valentine's Day?" Dan asked, a hint of a smile in his voice.

"I would love to go to dinner with you on Valentine's Day, Dan."

He picked me up at my apartment carrying a large bouquet of red roses. I was speechless. Red roses were a symbol of love, not merely friendship. I couldn't help wondering what Dan's thoughts were about me but I decided to just enjoy his company, take it one step at a time and see where that led.

We had an enjoyable dinner. The restaurant was cozy, its ambiance warmed by dimmed lights and candles on every table. I sat across from Dan, watching him and listening to his every word.

"I'm sorry it took me so long to call you," he said as he reached for my hand across the table.

"It's okay, I—."

"No, wait, let me finish, please," he interrupted. "Kelly came back to get all her belongings out of my house. She tried to get back with me hoping we could work things out and I was surprised to find that I had no feelings left for her. For the two years we were together she was the love of my life until she betrayed me and broke my heart. When I first met you, I was cautious because I didn't want to fall into the same trap. I believe I would never be able to get that close to anyone again, at least, not for a long time. I didn't want to go out with you while I was thinking of another woman, either, that wouldn't have been fair to you and that's why you haven't seen me." He squeezed my hand. "Maria, Kelly is out of my life and my thoughts. When I look at you, I think there's a chance that love will happen again, I'm willing to try."

Candlelight danced on his face and I found myself thinking I was as happy as I could ever be. All the doubts I had about never seeing him again just evaporated as I sensed the sincerity of what I was hearing.

Dan ordered a bottle of wine and when it was poured, he raised his glass and smiled. "To the future," he said. "Our future."

"To us," I responded smiling, then teased, "Does this mean your head is straightened out?"

"Yes, it is," he answered with conviction.

We were becoming more than just friends and I could tell by his relaxed manner and the tender and appreciative way he looked at me, that I was indeed special to him. We spent the evening getting to know each other better as he shared his past with me.

"I was born in Rimbey, Alberta, the first born of Marg and Victor Trautman. At a very young age when my parents divorced, I was sent to live at my grandparents' farm. My grandfather favoured me for reasons I don't know because my other two brothers, Richard and Dennis, were taken to foster homes. My mother took my sister Ginny with her and it wasn't until later in life that we all got together as a family. At the age of twenty-two, my grandfather gave me an old truck and I travelled to Ontario where I hoped to find a better life,"

"Were you not happy at the farm?" I asked.

"I didn't mind the farm but I was allergic to wheat and other grains we grew there, so I needed to live somewhere else and Ontario seemed to be a good destination."

I gave his hand a gentle squeeze. "I'm glad you decided to settle here, otherwise I would never have met you."

"So am I," he continued. "I found work in a carpet store as a stock boy. One day, an electrician came in to do some work and asked me if I'd help him pull some wires. I did of course and not long after that I started working with him as an apprentice. With much determination and hard work, I succeeded in building my own company in Newmarket.

He poured us some more wine. "Am I boring you, Maria?"

He looked at me with such tenderness that my heart was singing the sweetest symphony. "No, not at all. I love listening to you and I am so happy that you feel comfortable enough with me to tell me about your life. Please tell me more."

"I eventually met my ex-wife, Heather, and we got married. You met the fruits of that marriage already, but unfortunately it didn't work out for us and thirteen years later we divorced."

"What happened?" I wanted to know. "Did you love Heather when you married?"

"I thought I did, the first few years were good but I was busy working on my career, I wanted to succeed, to prove to myself that in spite of my humble beginnings, I could make it happen. I wanted to provide for my family and in order to do that, I needed to work hard. I was rarely home in time for dinner because I stayed late at work, catching up with all the paperwork because during the day, I was out, working."

Our pasts were similar in that we both had little love as children and we'd both worked hard to build a comfortable life. Through our conversation that night, we truly bonded.

Time flew. When I saw Dan look at his watch, my heart sank because I knew it was time to go. I wished we could have gone on talking forever but my heart floated again when he reached for my hand and held it as we walked back to his truck so he could take me home.

"Would you like to come up for a nightcap?" I asked, hopeful. I didn't want to part with him.

"I better not, I still have to drive home but I will walk you upstairs," he said, kissing me tenderly on the nose.

When we got to my apartment and before we had the chance to say goodnight, he kissed me. The first touch of his lips on mine is a sweet memory that will last forever. His arms tightened around me, pressing us together. I was almost paralyzed by the closeness of our bodies and the warmth of his breath. I grew lightheaded as the heat of our kisses rose, and then he stopped. As he pulled away from me, his voice was soft and passionate.

"I want you, Maria, I want you more than you could possibly know, but I don't want to rush it. I'll be taking cold showers for the next week but if I don't leave now, my self-control will be gone."

I was breathless and a little disappointed but I saw the reasoning. This was not a passing infatuation, I hoped this was the kind of love that's long lasting and satisfying. We kissed tenderly again, then said goodnight.

I didn't hear from him for a few days and the suspense was killing me. I missed him; it was as if part of my soul had left with him. My pride wouldn't allow me to be the one to get in touch so I hoped he would call me soon.

I spoke with Elizabeth several times during that week because she wanted me to keep her posted. If I didn't call her, she would call me. Unfortunately, neither of us had anything to share.

I continued to daydream about the last evening Dan and I had spent together. The memory of his sensual kiss elicited a delicious feeling that flooded through me each and every time those thoughts entered my mind. But our relationship, as wonderful as it was, had not been fully established. I could scarcely forget there was another woman out there who wanted him for herself. Tormented by those irritating thoughts, I came to the realization that I really had nothing to offer him, nothing but myself.

After a week of agony and nervous anticipation, the phone call finally arrived. I attempted to make my voice sound casual but my heart was beating so strong that I thought he could probably hear it on the other side of the line.

"I missed you," he said softly.

I loved hearing those words but at the same time I wanted to scream at him: *Why the hell did you keep me in suspense for the whole week? Why couldn't you have picked up the bloody phone?*

"I missed you too. How are you?" I kept my voice neutral, trying to sound as if I didn't care.

"I'm good, thanks. Hey, my daughters are coming this weekend and I was wondering if you'd come and visit? I want to make proper introductions."

I wanted to dance across the room at first but when I realized what he was asking, apprehension seized me. I envisioned Shelby's venomous look of revulsion at the mere sight of me. However, if I wanted to be with him, I would have to face the girl and let her know that I meant no harm and would love to be her friend. I could just imagine how she would react.

Nonetheless, I ventured, "Are you sure that's a good idea? Isn't it a bit too soon? I'm concerned how they'll react and I don't want to hurt them in any way."

"They're tough kids," Dan replied. "They will be fine and I want to see you."

"Well then, I would love to come up and visit with you and your children but please don't let them hurt me either, okay?" I said laughing

"Consider me your protector," he replied, laughing with me. "I shall not let the rebel children harm you in any way. Seriously, Maria, everything will be fine. I already spoke with Louisa and she will sleep in Claire's bedroom so you can have hers. It's all proper, don't worry about anything, just come up, please."

When I arrived at Dan's house in Newmarket the following Friday, he opened the front door for me and appeared to be alone. I took care to dress a little more conservative than usual, in a high neck blouse and a knee-length skirt. I wanted to appear mature and a little older because after all, Louisa was only fifteen years younger than me and, if by chance I ended up in a role of stepmother, I may as well start playing the part now.

"The children won't be here till tomorrow morning," Dan said, "I should have told you but I arranged it that way so you can have the chance to relax. And at the same time, we can also talk and be together without any interruptions. How about a glass of wine?"

"That will start it nicely," I said, laughing.

Dan walked into the kitchen and came back with a bottle of Cabernet and two glasses. He sat beside me and with wrists intertwined we cheered and took a sip, then he leaned over and gently kissed my lips.

"Would you like to go out to dinner with me, milady?" he asked, landing a kiss on my hand.

"Where are you taking me?"

"Upstairs...no, just kidding," he said with a naughty grin. "There is a very good restaurant nearby that I think you will like." He winked.

Sleep didn't come easily that first night in Dan's house. My mind raced with thoughts about what was happening in my life and how wonderful it was being with someone who respected me, someone I wanted to be with, someone with whom I may want to spend the rest of my life.

The next morning, Dan made a pot of coffee and we sat and waited for the girls to arrive. I wondered if they were excited to see me or if they didn't want me there.

"You look nervous—are you?" Dan asked.

"I can't lie. Yes, I am. I have never been in this situation before and I must admit that meeting your children in this capacity scares the hell out of me."

"Well, don't worry, my love, I have forewarned them about your visit this weekend so I trust they'll behave well and perhaps be very happy to see you, just as I am."

"Why is it that I am so apprehensive then?"

Shelby came in first. She didn't look at me or listen to her father as he reintroduced us, just went straight upstairs.

"Shelby come back here. Do you hear me? Come back down here and don't be rude," he peeked upstairs and repeated his command but his words were ignored. He turned to me. "She'll come around, don't mind her."

I didn't mind, I didn't know the girl and frankly, I recall thinking that I'd rather her not be around if she was going to behave like that.

"Louisa, you've met Maria before. She is going to stay the weekend and we're all going to have a good time getting acquainted."

"Hi, Louisa," I greeted with a little nod of my head.

"Hi, Maria, good to see you again," she nodded back.

"And I'm Claire, I am very pleased to see you again, Maria, and I'm glad you're here," the little one piped up as she gave me a big hug. That made me feel so much better, two out of three wasn't bad, I thought.

In the afternoon we decided to go for a walk in the park. The girls strolled in front of us while Dan and I walked behind them, chatting.

"I wonder why Shelby has such animosity towards me," I said, more to myself than to Dan.

"She's just a kid, she'll get over it. She acted the same way the first time she met Kelly. It's just how she is I suppose, very protective," Dan answered.

"Did she like Kelly? Did they get along?"

"She was okay with her; we did things as a family and I never really noticed any bad behaviour on her part."

"I guess it's me, then. Do you think she sees me as a threat? Maybe she thinks I'll take you away from her. Every time she sees me, I feel like I'm a bad smell to her."

"Agh, don't let her worry you, I am very happy that you're here and I know that eventually, she'll learn to accept you," he said reaching for my hand and kissing it. At that moment, Claire glanced back to see if anything else was going on besides walking. When she saw us holding hands, she immediately positioned herself between her sisters and covered her mouth, whispering to them as if she was telling a great secret, giggling and looking back at her father and me. Her sisters didn't turn back to witness the event or to validate Claire's observation, perhaps due to a stern warning from Shelby to not look. I didn't know what this girl saw in me that inspired such contempt but the few times I was with them, it seemed that she was the boss. The person who would have the last say and, in this case, the first say. "Don't turn around."

That evening I took charge of cooking dinner and with Dan's help, prepared a fantastic meal of pork chops, mashed potatoes and stuffed zucchini from Dan's garden. Louisa watched me quietly while I worked and smiled at me every time I looked in her direction, while little Claire wanted to be involved in everything that was going on. During dinner, Shelby showed a side of herself that surprised me, she was witty and funny and kept everyone laughing including me, although not once did she look in my direction. I laughed at her jokes because she was good. I wanted to be included in her audience, but she didn't acknowledge me. I thought her quite arrogant for one so young. Did she fear I would take her daddy away or did she want to be the only female in charge? I would bet on the latter.

When dinner was over and the dishes were done, we sat in the living room and watched some TV.

"Thanks for letting me sleep in your room, Louisa," I said to her, sitting beside me.

"Oh, that's not a problem, my pleasure," she replied, pleasantly.

I found it interesting that all three knew by now that their father and I were an item and two of them didn't have a problem with it. So, it couldn't be me, could it?

The next day was Sunday and back to reality. I made breakfast for everyone and before we knew it, there was a knock on the door.

"Mom's here." Claire let everyone know. I went to the door and by this time, Heather was by her car, ready to pile them in and get going.

I peeked out. "Good morning," I called out in a pleasant voice, "They're getting ready and will be out in a minute. I'm Maria, by the way."

"Good morning, Maria, I'm Heather, pleased to meet you," she said in an equally pleasant voice.

The girls rushed out and before she got into the car, little Claire waved. "Bye, Maria."

I watched the car disappear around the corner and turned to Dan, who was standing beside me and waiting for me to get into my own car.

"See you soon," he whispered with a smile.

"Call me," I replied as I got into my car and drove away.

I sat alone in my tiny apartment that evening, with a longing for Dan that both amazed and excited me. My thoughts of him and his daughters—even Shelby, whom I thought I could win over—filled me with a warm and comforting feeling, a feeling of home and family. This feeling sometimes came with doubts as well, but I tried to hide them, to tell myself that I could do this, I could love this family enough to make everyone happy, including myself.

Chapter Twenty

Trust, Distrust and Love

When the phone rang two days later and Dan invited me for the weekend again, I accepted.

"The girls won't be here, it'll be just you and me," he reported.

"Is that right?" I replied a bit sarcastically. "Was that arranged on purpose so we could be alone?"

"Damn right it was. I want to see you without having to worry about whether I should hold your hand or not."

"I see. What else do you have in mind?"

"I like your train of thought but my intentions are honourable—you'll be safe with me."

"Darn, and here I thought your intentions may be a little naughty."

Dan let that comment go untouched. "Hey, I play in the local baseball league, would you like to go with me and watch the game?"

"I like the way you change the subject but, yes, I would love to come and watch you play ball."

"That's great, I'll see you Friday."

Dan played baseball both in the Newmarket men's league as well as in the mixed league. That weekend the men were holding a tournament so I went with him and met all his friends and their wives who kept me company while the game was being played. They were very polite and friendly and I occasionally caught some of them casting curious glances my way. I would either pretend I didn't notice or sometimes I would acknowledge their glance with a smile. After the games were finished for the day, Dan and I celebrated our time together as a couple and went out for dinner. Because Dan had come to know that I love flowers, he surprised me with a beautiful pink orchid corsage which he pinned on me before we left the house. The gentle and caring way he did this little chore touched my heart.

"There, a beautiful flower for a beautiful girl," he said, looking at me with a tender smile.

The delicate orchid was set with a spray of baby's breath and a touch of greenery, finished off with a delicate cream coloured beaded ribbon. It was a unique work of beauty and I was deeply moved by Dan's thoughtfulness. Despite suffering from a cold, he was just as cheerful, polite and attentive as he always was in my company.

When the evening ended and we returned to Dan's house, he tried to keep a healthy distance from me, not wanting to infect me with his cold.

"Good night my dear. Guess I better go to bed and try to get rid of this cold. Have a good night's sleep," he said as he walked upstairs and out of sight.

"Good night, feel better."

I lay in Louisa's bed for a very long time, unable to sleep. I could hear Dan coughing in his bed and my heart went out to him. I wanted to hold him in my arms and comfort him but knew that by doing that, I would be changing everything between us. Was that what I wanted?

Absolutely, I thought as I got out of bed.

I knocked on his door.

"Come in," he said.

I didn't say a word, just went to his bed and slipped in beside him. He wrapped his arms around me and we lay close to each other. After a while it seemed he might fall asleep so I kissed his lips gently, ready to go to sleep myself. To my surprise he kissed me back once, twice, again and again until I lost count. My pulse pounded under his gentle touch and I tasted the tenderness of his kisses. I knew in my heart that he loved me.

"Should I stop?" he asked, his voice a little husky.

He must have known that if he did stop, I would die. His hands roamed freely over me, exploring, brushing my skin with fire. All the ardour that had been bottled up between us was now released and I didn't want this night to end. I didn't care about sleep, all I cared about was being there, in the arms of this man who loved me as a person and as a woman.

The following morning as we parked by the ball diamond, he covered my hand with his and sighed, sounding a little sad.

"After last night," he began, "I feel I must be totally honest with you, Maria. It's important that you know that I can never give you a child. I had a vasectomy a few years ago."

I looked away, silenced by the gravity of what he was saying.

"If this is not what you want, Maria, now's the time to make a decision."

I tried to focus on what he had just said. I knew I should say something but as my mouth started forming the words, his finger touched my lips.

"Don't say anything right now," he said quietly. "Think about it for a while." Then he kissed me, got out of the truck and headed over to join the team.

I watched his back as he walked away and asked myself how much I wanted to be with this man. What would life be like without him now that I had found him? Would I end up regretting not having any children of my own? I was almost thirty-one years old and he was thirty-nine.

In the past, whenever I tried to envision my future, I always thought I would love to have a family of my own. But I also thought that if I didn't have children by the time I was thirty, I wouldn't have any. If I had any children, I would want them to have all my attention and love, I wanted to raise them and see them grow up while I was still young. It had been a long time since I'd made that little deal with myself. Was I only recalling it now because I didn't want to give Dan up? I also had to consider his daughters in this equation. Would they accept me into their lives? Would I be a good stepmother?

Dan was fast becoming the best part of my life and, when I was with him, I was content with my life. By the end of the game, I decided I wouldn't let the question of babies worry me that day.

And yet, in the hours and days that followed, doubt crept back into my mind. The more I thought about it, the more doubts pushed into my heart. Maybe I was just infatuated with him because no other man had ever treated me as he did, maybe Kelly would come back and he would want her, instead of me.

On the other hand, I believed I was where God wanted me to be at that very moment and if He meant for Dan and me to be together, then we would be. I had to trust in Him.

We had a quiet dinner at his home that evening and were talking at the kitchen table when the phone rang. I had no idea who it was at first, but it soon became clear.

Dan's cheeks flushed and he started speaking nervously "Yes? Uh-huh. All right. Okay."

He lowered his voice and faced the wall and I suddenly felt like an intruder on a private conversation. I left the room and went upstairs to pack my overnight bag.

When I came downstairs with my bag in hand, he was no longer on the phone. He didn't volunteer any information about his phone conversation and I didn't ask for any, nor did he inquire as to why I was leaving.

"I'll call you during the week," he said as he walked me to the door.

"Yep, bye," I manage, in spite of the gloom enfolding me.

On my way home, I tried to deal with my disappointment.

I slept with the man and met his kids, so what? He never made me any promises, never told me I was the love of his life, what right did I have to be upset? I spent a very quiet week and when the phone rang on Thursday evening, my hand lingered over the receiver and I wondered if I should ignore it.

No, I had to know where I stood with him. I had to know if Kelly was back.

"Hi, Maria, am I going to see you this weekend?"

"Are you sure you want to see me?"

"Of course, I do, what kind of question is that? Don't you want to see me?"

"I do, but how about you come down and visit with me here?"

"I thought you'd bring that up at some point, but the truth is, I feel claustrophobic in that little apartment."

"All right, I'll see you on Friday evening."

I tried to rationalize my predicament. It's not like we're engaged, he can see whomever he wants and so can I, but the thing is, I don't want to be with a man who feels he can see anyone he wants. I don't want him to think that I'm okay with this, but what right do I have to question him? And what would I ask?

I decided I would let it go for now. I didn't know what happened nor did I want to.

The subject was never mentioned by either one of us and Dan was attentive and loving as he had been before. I decided to forget about the whole thing.

The following weekend, we had resumed our routine and everything seemed to be as good as it had been before the phone call. However, at two a.m. on Saturday night, while Dan and I were lovingly entwined in a warm embrace just after a sensual session of lovemaking, the damn phone rang. The same muffled conversation as he turned away from me.

What the hell was going on? Again, I didn't say a word but simply removed myself from his bed and went into Louisa's bedroom.

The next morning, I was the first one downstairs. I turned the coffee on and made myself busy cleaning the counters and the stove.

"Good morning, Maria," Came a cheerful greeting from upstairs.

"Good morning," I responded, casually.

He must've sensed the chill in my voice because he came up to me and embraced me from behind, planting a kiss on my neck.

"I'm sorry about the phone call last night," he said, "It was Kelly."

I feigned surprise. "Really? You don't say," I reacted, turning around and waiting for an explanation.

"She still has some of her stuff in this house and she wondered when she could come and pick it up."

"Did she have to call you at two in the morning to ask you that?" I asked, unable to mask the annoyance in my voice.

"I'm sorry, Maria, but she sounded upset. She broke up with her boyfriend and I didn't have the heart to hang up on her."

"Ah, she broke up with her boyfriend," I said. "And I imagine now that she is a single woman again, she wants you back." My gut clenched. Just as I had thought, Kelly was alone again and she was coming after my man.

At 11:00 in the morning while we sat in the living room, the phone rang again and it was Kelly. This time he had a conversation with her about the co-ed baseball league. I assumed the call was a ploy just so she could talk with Dan.

"How are you? Yes, we are. Actually, yes. Of course, we can always use another woman on our team."

I didn't need any coaching. I rose, picked up my purse and went out the back door. I got into my car, slammed the door and burned the grass on the way out. I sped down Highway 400 towards Toronto, hardly able to see the road for the tears. I was crushed— humiliated. I probably shouldn't even have been driving but I didn't care. My fury and disappointment overshadowed all rational and sensible thinking. Maybe I would die. That would be all right because then my misery would end. I should have known better than to let this man bewitch me with all his charm, gentlemanly manners and family introductions.

What a fool I had been. He seemed so comfortable speaking with her, like it was a natural everyday occurrence. And my heart was breaking into a thousand pieces. I mistakenly presumed I was now the love of his life but this woman, Kelly, or whatever her name was, still seemed to have an immense influence over him. Only time would tell what would happen and meanwhile, I would stay away from that phone.

On April 20, 1984, I would have celebrated my thirty-first birthday if I didn't have a broken heart. I spent the morning doing something I hadn't done in a long time: crying. Crying an endless cascade of tears. All my previous insecurities erupted and enveloped me like a tightly swaddled infant, while the shackles of the past tightened their grip around my heart. I do not dwell in self-pity. Every time my world is turned upside down, I push the bad memories away but, on this day, my mind was too distraught to cope.

Elizabeth came over in the morning to wish me a happy birthday.

"You look awful, what's wrong?

"It's over between Dan and I," I said. The tears were threatening again.

"Maria, my dear, why are you saying that? What has Danny done?"

"Nothing, and that's the point. Kelly phones him every time I visit, as if she knows I'm there and she can push me away. I'm tired of it, Elizabeth."

"Don't worry, my dear, he'll call," she said, but her voice didn't carry its usual confidence.

"I don't want him to call," I said sadly. "I never want to hear from him again—nothing good can come out of this relationship."

"He's a good man, Maria," she assured me, "and a very successful one. Kelly's romance didn't work out and she probably just realized her mistake. Now she wants him back."

As I hear my friend utter these words, the flood of tears started all over again and even though Elizabeth had me locked in a loving embrace, I couldn't help but feel like the most miserable person on this earth.

"She can have him, as long as he leaves me alone." I declared, tears streaming down my cheeks.

I wished Elizabeth would leave and let me wallow in my misery but it was a while before she said her goodbyes. After that, I found I had no more tears. They seemed to be frozen deep inside of me, I was utterly numb. The phone rang at three o'clock and I answered it thinking Elizabeth was checking up on me again.

"Hello?" I said miserably.

"Can a man take his girl out for dinner on her birthday?"

I couldn't believe it. "What about Kelly?" I asked.

"Maria, I loved Kelly very much. She was my life and I was very hurt when she left me, but she doesn't mean anything to me now. It's you I want, Maria. I love you and miss you."

Oh, the turmoil in my head. He sounded so sincere and yet.... I forced a recall of his words back through my head so I could find some kind of anchor. "It's you I want, I love you," he had said.

"I missed you too," I finally uttered, though I wasn't ready to proclaim my love for him. Not after what he'd put me through. In the end, I agreed to go to dinner with him and he took me to the same restaurant where we celebrated our first date on Valentine's Day.

"I wanted to call you, I was dying to talk with you but I also wanted to end it with Kelly once and for all, so she wouldn't come between us ever again."

"I do want to believe you," I said, "but you sounded so contented talking on the phone with her, I couldn't help but think you were still in love with her."

"Well, she's in the past now," he said as he firmly but tenderly held my hand across the table. "All I want is to be with you, to go through this life with you, do you understand?"

"Yes, I understand." We both stood up and sealed the moment with a kiss.

He sounded so sincere that I wanted to suspend that moment in time. The way he looked at me with such love filled my heart, repairing all the damage it had undergone.

As poor and unimportant, as plain and scarred as I may have once been, I found someone who truly loved me. Someone who didn't care where I came from or how pitiful my life had been, or that I had nothing tangible to offer back, only myself.

But one thing I knew with absolute certainty at this crossroads of my life, I was the happiest girl in the universe and I would try to keep it that way, forever.

Chapter Twenty-One

Come What May

I will remember and cherish forever my first Christmas with Dan
and his children. Dan took care of cooking the turkey—which was to
become an annual tradition—and I helped with the remainder of the
meal. The girls were in charge of cleaning up afterwards and the
evening was happy and relaxed—except for Shelby. It was as clear
as a freshly cleaned window on a sunny day that she was not happy
with my intrusion in her father's house. I decided that I needed to
talk with the girl and soften things up between us, even though I felt
a lot of trepidation about doing so. Immediately after the kitchen
clean up, the obstinate Shelby went up to her room without a word to
anyone. She had seemed relaxed during dinner, carrying on with her
shenanigans and making everyone laugh, and as I headed upstairs, I

hoped she had retained some of that humour.

I knocked on the bedroom door but there was no answer. I knocked once more and gently turned the knob. Shelby lay on the bed with her nose in a book. I entered the room and closed the door behind, as she dragged her eyes from the book to look up at me and immediately returning her attention to the book again.

"Shelby, I would like to talk with you for a few minutes, is that okay?"

No answer or anything to indicate agreement.

"Shelby, I would really like for us to be friends."

She gave me a contemptuous look as she briefly fixed her eyes on me and then lowered her head and returned back to the book.

"I'm not here to take your dad from you, Shelby. On the contrary, I hope that someday we can be a happy family, together."

I could still not elicit a response from her or get any sign of acknowledgement that I had even spoken, so I sat at the edge of the bed and waited. She rolled her body as far away from me as she could while remaining on the bed with the book still in her hands.

"I'm told I'm a nice girl, friendly and sincere. Won't you give me a chance?"

A page turned, even though I was sure she was not reading anything.

"Well, Shelby, I'm here to stay, whether it pleases you or—.

"That wasn't my choice!" she shouted as she turned to face me, an angry look on her young face.

I tried to remain calm. "I understand and respect your feelings but your dad and I love each other. I'm not going anywhere, Shelby, I thought I would make things easier for everyone by offering my friendship. I hope with time you will see me as a friend, someone who cares about you and your sisters. Be part of my family, Shelby, and I will be part of yours."

I got up from the bed and quietly left the room but I wasn't happy that I had to try so hard to please this determined and spoiled kid without any positive results. On the contrary, now I knew for certain that she didn't like me and would likely never accept me.

By January of 1986, over two years into our relationship, Dan and I had settled into a routine that made me wonder where our relationship was going. Most of the time I drove to Newmarket because of Dan's overwhelming claustrophobia whenever he spent any significant time in my apartment. I didn't mind being the one to travel, getting out of the city and into a quaint town like Newmarket was quite refreshing, but the travel was not the issue. Dan had not shown any sign or made any promise of a commitment to me, other than his declaration of love. I loved him and knew in my heart of hearts that he returned my love, but that was no longer enough for me. I could still lose myself in the glorious pleasure of his touch, his graciousness and gentleness were like a ray of sunshine on a murky downcast day, yet, if he wasn't ready to make a serious commitment, then I would have to reconsider my life with him. I was no longer content to continue to allow our romance to float aimlessly. My heart would break to part ways after all we'd gone through, but I hungered for more commitment. I had to think of my future which I envisioned being in a totally and unconditionally loving relationship with someone. My future included a happy marriage and children, and even though Dan's girls were not my own flesh and blood, I was ready to embrace them.

One cold and snowy winter morning in January 1986, after Dan had delivered the girls to their mother's house, I brought up the subject of our relationship and my expectations. He had just poured two glasses of wine and we sat in the living room, looking out into the yard and watching the snowflakes weave a white carpet on the frozen ground, enjoying the quiet.

"Dan, are you happy with our relationship?" I asked looking for his reaction.

His eyes widened at my question and he turned to face me. "Of course, I'm very happy with our relationship. Why do you ask, is something wrong?" he asked, setting his glass on the coffee table.

"No, but I have been thinking that we have known each other for over two years and there has been no indication of a commitment from you. I feel secure in your love for me, Dan, but do you ever think of the future?" I asked turning to him and looking into his eyes. "Do you ever think of giving marriage another chance, Dan?"

"That's a heavy one for a Sunday afternoon," he said as he reached for my hand. "I guess we should talk about it, if it means that much to you."

"It does mean that much to me. Tell you what, Dan," I said, squeezing his hand and looking into the depths of his blue eyes. "Let's take a month and think about it. I will understand if you decide not to make a commitment, but I need to know where I stand with you, is that fair?"

He started to say something but I stopped him, putting the tip of my finger to his lips. "Don't say anything right now, let's both think about it and get together in a month's time."

I got up from the sofa and set my empty glass on the table, then kissed him and went home.

On the way home, I vowed to be strong and stay away from Newmarket so I would not influence his decision.

One week to the day, Dan called and asked if I would come up and visit.

"I miss you," he said, "I need to see you."

As I heard his words, a feeling of elation came over me, I couldn't wait to see him.

When I stepped through the doorway, he was waiting for me, holding two glasses of white wine.

"Please sit down, Maria. We have to talk."

I loved this man more than I had ever loved anyone or anything in my life. I would either end up going home alone today, or he would remain the love of my life.

I hoped I was prepared either way.

We sat down—he on his chair and me on the sofa—and he turned to me. "You know, you really surprised me when you gave me your ultimatum."

"I know. I apologize but for me it was necessary."

He nodded his head gently. "I understand, it's me who should be apologizing. I thought about what you said very seriously and I couldn't bear it if I didn't have you in my life."

He took both my hands in his as he knelt on the soft carpet before me and opened a little box that contained an engagement ring. "Maria, will you marry me?"

His eyes were so deep and intense, I thought I might melt right into them. A tear escaped and slipped down my cheek as he slid the ring on my finger. We stood up and I wrapped my arms around his neck as we kissed.

"Yes," I whispered. "It'll be a privilege and a pleasure to be your wife."

I was the happiest woman in the world. The fact that I would never have any children of my own didn't matter because I loved him and I felt my love for him far surpassed that of having a biological child. I would do my best to help him raise his own children and somehow, someday, I was determined we would become a real family. It saddened me that Shelby was so unfriendly but I hoped she'd come around. I would simply try to be her friend and hope that someday she would see me differently.

Dan and I agreed that it didn't make any sense for me to live in Toronto any longer. We decided we should live together for a little while before we got married to make sure this was what we both wanted. I continued working in Toronto but now that I lived in Newmarket, sometimes the drive was very challenging, especially at the end of the day on a rainy or snowy night. Dan didn't want me working so far away, either. One day he told me he didn't care who cooked dinner but he hated eating alone. I had to think seriously about finding a job in Newmarket so I would be closer to home. When I started looking, there were lots of jobs I could have taken but none of them offered a secure and solid future.

Dan knew a lot of people in his town and knowing I was getting nowhere on my own, spoke with some people at the Health Department. Before I knew it, I was called for an interview and hired to work in the school health services. This entailed getting to know all the schools in the region, making sure every child was properly immunized and keeping records. It was all new to me but with my previous work experience and dealing with people, I was soon making progress and enjoying my new job.

When Dan and I began talking about a date for our wedding, I told him I hoped to be married in June, which was a popular month for weddings.

"June is when I go on most of my fishing trips," he teased. "You're not trying to change me already, are you?"

"I wouldn't dream of it," I replied, amused. "How's July? I could settle for July."

"July sounds fine to me."

"It's a date then. I'll start planning."

I decided to approach George Lacasse and ask if he would give me away, since he and Elizabeth had matched us up in the first place.

George was delighted that I considered him for the position normally filled by the father of the bride. His eyes crinkled as he gave me a warm smile and said, "Honey, I would be honoured and proud to walk you down the aisle to your Dan." He then pulled me close and gave me a fatherly hug, kissing the top of my head.

Elizabeth's smile was happy when she opened her arms to embrace me. "I am so happy for you, dear Maria, and so proud that you and our Danny have decided to settle down, finally."

These two wonderful people were so dear to me.

Friends who are family made me think about my own family here in Canada. I didn't keep in touch with them on a regular basis however, I decided to invite them to my wedding. Not so much for my uncle, but for my aunt and cousins, I wanted them there.

Robyn and I were still the best of friends and we still got together whenever our busy lives permitted. I decided to ask her if she would be my matron of honour. She accepted.

I invited Louisa, Shelby and Claire to be my bridesmaids. I wanted Dan's daughters to be happy for their father and be part of the wedding celebration. I was about to formally enter their lives and wanted us to be a family together.

"Do we get to call you Mom?" Claire enquired when I got them together.

"You can call me anything you want, sweetheart, as long as it's good and not insulting," I said as I hugged the little girl.

"I wouldn't do that. I'm glad you're marrying Dad," she replied.

"Thanks, Claire, it's good to hear."

"When are you guys getting married?" Louisa asked.

"Well, I always wanted to get married in June but your dad says that's when he goes fishing so I settled for July."

"What? He won't get married in June because he's going fishing? Why am I not surprised? That's my dad," Louisa said, laughing.

"No, I understand and I don't mind, I know he loves to do it and I wouldn't want to change anything," I said.

"Yeah, but what's more important? You should've stuck to your plans, Maria, and told him it would be June or nothing." She now laughed hysterically knowing very well that wouldn't go over well with her dad. All of a sudden, we were all laughing, caught in the moment and imagining Dan facing a determined me.

All except Shelby, who looked totally bored but managed to nod when I asked her if she would join her sisters as my bridesmaid.

Our search for a wedding venue led us to a charming chapel at Black Creek Pioneer Village. Dan was not a religious person so we agreed to have a non-denominational service. We met the chaplain and set our wedding day for July 5th, 1986 and to add a special touch to the day, we arranged for a horse-drawn carriage to take me from the village gate to the chapel.

Time went by in a blur. I used every free moment to organize our big day, wanting everything to be perfect. Robyn was living in a nearby town with her husband, Howie, and she did whatever she could to help me. We booked the venue for the reception, shopped for my wedding dress and all the attendants' dresses, and Dan's daughters offered their assistance with some of the other preparations such as the music, the flowers, and all the special things that would make our day a happy one.

Dan's best buddy, Frank, was the best man, and Howie and our friend Keith were the other ushers.

We got a rehearsal appointment with the chaplain and took everyone out to dinner afterwards to celebrate.

The day before the wedding, Frank took Dan up to his property to go fishing but promised me he would have my groom at the church on time. Robyn spent the night with me and treated me to a bubble bath and champagne. We talked and laughed the entire evening, mostly about our belly dancing days and our hopes for the future. Finally, at two o'clock in the morning we decided to call it a night and get some sleep, otherwise we would be the ones arriving late at the chapel

Chapter Twenty-Two

Fulfilled Dreams

July 5, 1986 was our wedding day and the happiest day of my life. On this day, the whole house vibrated with excitement.

Dan's mom and some of his relatives flew in from Alberta for our wedding and I invited my aunt, uncle and cousins. It had been a few years since I lived with them and although I had not forgiven my uncle for putting me in such a situation that shamed me, I had long ago swept that dirt under the carpet so I wouldn't lose touch with my aunt and cousins.

My aunt had been the leading influence at my coming to Canada and if it hadn't been for her, I would never had met the love of my life. I loved my aunt dearly and I long ago decided I would always try to be there for her, as she was there for me when I most needed help.

The girls looked beautiful.

I bought them knee-length pink dresses and took them all to the beauty salon with Robyn and me, that morning.

George looked very handsome in his black tuxedo and as soon as he arrived, he took my hands in his and told me I was a beautiful bride. Robyn looked radiant, even though she was six months pregnant with her first baby. That baby later became my goddaughter, Hilary.

It was a perfect day. Everything unfolded better than I had ever dreamed of in my deepest of dreams. The girls passed me in the living room, heading outside to their waiting car and I smiled at all of them and gave them a thumbs-up. My day became even more perfect when I caught Shelby smiling back at me.

I travelled to the church in a limousine with Robyn and George.

George had made sure there was a bottle of Dom Perignon in the limo and as we started on our way, he handed both of us a glass and raised his own.

"Here's to you and Dan, Maria. May your marriage be long and happy. Remember that Elizabeth and I will always support and love you both."

As I hugged my friend, I said, "Thank you for being such a special part of my life and thank you for this day. It would never have happened if it wasn't for you and Elizabeth."

"You're marrying a very special man," he said.

"But he's marrying a very special woman as well," Robyn added.

"Let's drink to that," George said, lifting his glass to us, "Cheers."

George and Robyn assisted me when we reached the village's gate. The horse-drawn carriage was waiting and ready for us with the driver dressed so professionally in formal wear. Both my friends helped me into the carriage and once we were all situated in the vehicle, the slow ride to the chapel began.

As we rounded the corner and the chapel building came into view, I committed every precious detail of this day to my memory. The rhythmic clip-clop of the horse's hooves and the sound of the carriage wheels against the pavement, the soft gentle breeze that whispered through the trees as we rode under the giant oaks majestically lining both sides of the narrow road. The vibrant summer flowers in the many small gardens throughout the grounds—it all seemed like a fairy tale. The picturesque setting was the perfect place on earth for our special event on this glorious day.

I was the happiest I had ever been. Yes, the terrible trauma in my past had threatened to overpower me many times, but I worked through it and emerged stronger and learned many of life's lessons. I was confident and happy and refused to let my past hold me back. This was my day of victory against all the negativity that had forever overshadowed my existence.

As if sensing my reminiscing, George's gentle squeeze of my hand helped me keep my emotions under control. I focussed my attention to the outside of the chapel and saw my girls were already there, waiting for me.

Claire, Shelby and Louisa started the procession, followed by Robyn.

As I walked down the aisle on George's arm, his large hand covering my small one for reassurance and support, I looked at all the friends and family who had come to witness this momentous event. Some of the faces beamed with joy while some looked at me with bright and teary eyes. I smiled at these friends who had come to support two people who had found love in each other, Dan and me. My smiling groom stood near the altar, waiting patiently with his attendants and the chaplain. When we all completed our journey down the aisle, George gave my hand to Dan and then took his seat beside Elizabeth.

The ceremony began and when all the vows were said, my life changed forever and my heart sang.

I became a complete and blessed woman.

I believed God and the universe had granted me this day because of the fervour I put in every prayer when I wished for happiness. I didn't know how smooth or rocky the future might be but as long as I had Dan by my side, I was confident I could overcome any obstacles.

He was my love, my life, my whole existence. As I walked out of the chapel with my husband, in my mind I saw my grandmother's image, so clear and smiling as if telling me that everything will be okay now. She appeared as a ray of shining light, beckoning to me and embracing me with love which I felt in the depths of my heart.

Thank you, Grandma, I will never forget you.

As my husband guided me into the sunshine, we stopped and accepted congratulations from our family and friends.

This happy occasion would live in my mind forever and as our friends applauded our union, I vowed to celebrate life, always.

The reception was catered and a disc jockey entertained our guests. Many would say years later that it was the best party they had ever gone to. To me, it was a fairy tale wedding and I was the princess who had found her prince.

Chapter Twenty-Three

Going Back

Almost fifteen years had passed since I'd left Portugal to seek my future in Canada. So much had happened since then. I was a completely different person from the little girl I'd once been. When Dan asked where I would like to go for our honeymoon, Portugal was the first place that came to mind. Dan's best man, Frank, and his wife, Marg, had never seen the country and asked if they could go with us. We enjoyed their company and had in fact gone on vacation with them several times in the past, so it was an easy request to accept.

During the long flight over the Atlantic, Dan snoozed comfortably beside me but I found it hard to do the same. Instead, I used the quiet to reminisce a bit about my life, past and present. I had been corresponding with my mother and told her about our plans. She sent me a letter after that (probably written by my sister) and I was surprised by her amiability

"When are you coming? I'm looking forward to seeing you and meeting your husband and friends," she had said. "I told your siblings you were visiting and they are also very excited to see you."

I wanted to see Paulo and Ana again, though I only remembered them as children. I remembered how I had often been left in charge of them, and how my half-sister had resented my half-brother when he first came home. I remembered the anxious look on my half-sister's little face, anytime my mother and stepfather fought. How she ran to me looking for answers I didn't have. All of these memories reminded me of my mother's cruelty and I was amazed to discover that my heart held no grudges against her.

Fragments of my life echoed through my mind, transporting me back to the beginning of my earliest memories, to the endless stories I heard from Aunt Licinia, my grandma, and occasionally from my mother as well.

I gazed at my handsome and sleeping husband and smiled, feeling calm and safe. Eventually I closed my eyes and willed myself to sleep, drifting into a world of dreams.

I conjured up the image of my mother, hastily racing home through a wild and angry storm one fateful night, pregnant with the seed of a man who had stolen her innocence. And when his wife discovered his deceit, my mother was thrown into the cold night. Scared and feeling terribly alone, her life in ruins and her dreams viciously crushed, she ran home to the comfort of her mother's arms.

The dream came to an abrupt halt at the sound of the pilot announcing the plane's descent into Lisbon. Jolted awake, I heard the crew announce that the local time was six in the morning. I glanced at my watch and noted it was then midnight in Canada.

During the taxi ride to Hotel Tivoli, I looked at every building and every street name. Although it all seemed vaguely familiar, it also felt as if the memories were from another lifetime. The girl who had left Portugal all those years ago, the young girl so full of hope and yet so lonesome, was now a happy and married woman with many cherished friends. I would never forget how I struggled not to succumb to desperation and surrender to an empty life, in this beautiful city.

Heavy with jet lag, all we wanted was to get to the hotel and have a nap.

After breakfast the next day, I called my mother to tell her we had arrived and were planning on visiting them for the day before we set off on our exploration of Portugal. My stepfather answered the phone and his friendliness took me by surprise.

"It's good to hear from you, we have been expecting your call."

"Thank you. We are planning on coming to see you but I need your address," I said. I didn't have their summer address. My stepfather still stopped at the old apartment to pick up the mail once in a while, but mostly they lived at the beach at this time of the year.

"Tell me where you are and I will come and get you right away, are you at the airport?"

"Oh no, we are at the Hotel Tivoli," I told him.

"You're at the hotel already? When did you arrive?"

"Last evening, "I replied.

"You have been here all this time and just called now? You're a bad girl. Not to worry, I will pick you and your friends up within the hour, wait for me at the door."

I realized he was still the commanding man I remembered, only now he was a lot friendlier and I had no reason to be afraid of him.

We made our way to the lobby and a short while later I immediately recognized my stepfather when I saw a little man with white hair and beard climbing out of a small car.

Age had not slowed his gait and he walked briskly towards the hotel, smiling when he spotted us. He hugged me enthusiastically and kissed my cheeks. After shaking hands with everyone as I made introductions, he then opened the doors to his car and told us to get in, saying he wanted to take us to the beachfront where they kept a trailer by the water.

I translated my companion's endless questions for my stepfather. He tried to describe everything we passed, providing us with a brief history of the area. We travelled along Avenida da Liberdade, driving in downtown Lisbon and heading to the April 25th Bridge over the Tagus River. As we crossed the bridge, my companions all uttered sounds of admiration as the magnificent statue of Christ the King dominated the horizon, standing tall with outstretched arms as if embracing the city and everyone in it. We had seen the statue in the distance from the streets of Lisbon but not like this, in its breathtaking splendour.

Once on the other side of the river, we followed the narrow-cobbled streets of Trafaria until my stepfather came to a stop in front of a large wooden gate surrounded by tall stone walls. He got out of the car and told us he would be back shortly.

"Does your family live here?" Marg asked.

"I don't know," I replied.

A few minutes later my stepfather returned. In his left hand, two snow-white rabbits dangled by their hind legs, wriggling madly.

"Oh, my dear Lord. What do we have here?" Marg exclaimed, slapping her hand over her mouth.

My stepfather pointed at the rabbits, grinning with a proud expression.

I smiled and shook my head. "That's dinner, folks."

"Good. We'll have an old-fashioned rabbit stew," said Frank, laughing.

"Sounds good to me," Dan replied.

My stepfather went back through the large door and reappeared a short time later holding a brown package. The rabbits were now food. I winced as he sat behind the wheel and passed me the package.

He grinned, and looked pleased with himself.

"Were you surprised?" he asked, eyebrows lifted. "You always liked rabbit and I thought this would be a wonderful treat for you."

"Um, yes. It's a great treat, I was just surprised because I didn't expect to see them alive," I stammered. "But thank you, that's very thoughtful of you, we all like rabbit stew."

After getting over the shock of seeing the rabbits alive, even Marg nodded appreciatively. At this, my stepfather smiled, put the car in gear and headed for home.

We were now outside Trafaria and I recognized the road to Costa da Caparica. The ocean glittered and we saw people erecting tents on the beaches where they would take refuge when the sun got too hot to bear. When we finally reached our destination, my stepfather turned onto a sandy path that was barely wide enough for the car and parked it in front of a big trailer.

A woman stepped out of the trailer carrying a large platter of food which she set on a table under the canopy. As she turned to walk towards us, I stared, mesmerized by the look of her. She looked nothing like the woman I remembered. The woman I remembered was taller, proud and commanding, a force to be reckoned with. I expected she would've changed but not to this degree. This woman was a shadow of her former self. She still looked good for her age but hardly compared to the frightening person I remembered. Thick glasses made her eyes look huge, but her demeanour was the biggest surprise.

Her wide smile travelled to each one of us. And then her arms opened as she reached for me and I let her enfold me and kiss both my cheeks with affection. I opened my heart and returned my mother's embrace. We would never have the mother-daughter love and closeness, but I would settle for this. Better late than never, I concluded. She took a step back to look at me.

"You look beautiful," she said.

"Thanks...Mom," I managed.

After introducing her to my friends and husband, my stepfather insisted we sit and enjoy our meal. The platters were filled with large prawns, clams, and all sorts of Portuguese finger foods, including pasteis de bacalhau (cod cakes) and pasteis de camarao (shrimp cakes). There was also a large platter of dessert pastries. I could see they'd gone to a lot of expense to welcome us.

As we ate and talked, I ventured glances over at my mother. The closer I looked, the more I could see my first assessment was right. Diabetes had not been kind to her and likely her sight had deteriorated due to lack of treatment and poor diet. She was a lot thinner than I remembered and the weary lines of her face made her look much older than her fifty-six years. Once in a while she would also look at me and a smile brightened her face.

After the lunch dishes had been washed—which Dan and Frank volunteered to do—Marg and I talked with my mother and stepfather for some time.

"You have a lovely spot here," Marg commented, looking out to the sea.

I translated and my mother responded.

"Thank you. We have an apartment in the city but it serves only to house my husband during the week when he is working. He comes here on the weekends and this is also where I live now, no stairs and no walking on the hilly streets of Lisbon."

"Beautiful beach, great weather, I don't blame you."

After the dishes were done, the four of us excused ourselves and left to explore the area. My mom and stepfather gave us their blessing and encouraged us to go.

"Don't rush, dinner won't be for another couple of hours," my stepfather called after us.

The sand was too hot under our bare feet so we walked along the water's edge, enjoying the cool kiss of the water as it lapped against our legs. Seeing some children digging in the wet sand by a large rock, we approached, curious.

"What are you children digging for, what's in the bucket?" I asked, crouching down to a little girl's level.

"We're digging for clams," she responded, tilting the bucket so we could look into it.

"Good luck, then," I said as we waived to all of them and continued on our way.

We returned to the trailer just as my half-sister Ana arrived with her husband Miguel and daughter, Joana. It was an emotional reunion; I had not seen my little sister since she was eight years old. She was twenty-three years old and happily married. She'd had her baby girl and lived in an apartment away from her parents.

"Do you know what I missed, Lourdes?" she asked, "I missed having you here when I was growing up, I missed having an older sister to guide me, someone I could confide in."

"I understand," I said. "But you know I had to leave. Going to Canada was the best thing that ever happened to me and even though I missed you and Paulo, I knew I had to get away from our mother."

She pulled me towards her and hugged me tight. "I know you did, but I still missed you."

My heart filled with pride for my little sister. She had turned out to be a lovely person: warm, affectionate, and very articulate. She told me she had graduated from college as a computer operator.

I couldn't help remembering my mother's reaction when I'd said I wanted to enrol in evening classes to continue my education. Her words still stung: "I never went to school. You don't need to, either." Perhaps I paved the way for Ana's education.

My half-brother arrived shortly after we got back and I hugged and kissed him with affection. He was eighteen years old and very good looking, tall, brown hair and eyes and a friendly smile. The last time I'd seen him he'd been just a child. It filled me with pride, seeing him as a man. I later learned that he had followed in his father's footsteps and drove a truck for a living.

Dinner was tasty and I think we all tried to forget about the bunnies. As we sat around a large table that had been set up, the atmosphere was friendly. My friends and husband talked with my sister who knew a bit of English and when needed, I would translate. As my mother served dinner, she asked for my plate first. I watched as she carefully looked for the best piece of meat to put on my plate. There are no words that I can possibly use to describe my feelings as she so tenderly set the plate in front of me. All I could say was,

"Thank you."

After dinner we said our goodbyes and my stepfather took us back to our hotel. We agreed to see them again in two weeks, just prior to our return to Canada.

We wanted to drive south and visit Algarve, stopping at various sites along the way. To get the best of our visit, we hired a car and a driver with knowledge of both Portuguese history and the best places to go. It turned out we couldn't have found a better guide. He knew all the anecdotes of the areas and our group listened attentively to him every time we entered a church or climbed the stone steps of an ancient castle.

When we finally arrived in Algarve it was late afternoon, but the beaches were still bustling with people. We booked rooms at one of the hotels overlooking the beach and Marg and I went up to unpack. A few moments later she knocked on my door and tugged me towards the balcony. I followed her pointing finger and saw she was pointing at our husbands. At first, I didn't know what she thought was so unusual, but after watching the men for a few moments, I understood and laughed out loud. Our men were strolling side by side along the beach, hands clasped behind their backs, dark sunglasses hiding their eyes and nonchalantly admiring every topless beauty they came across.

We spent a glorious week playing on the beach and touring Faro, enjoying its many outdoor cafes, castles, and historical monuments. When we returned to Lisbon, we took my family out for dinner and Dan proved to Frank once and for all, that it took more than thirteen olives to acquire a taste for them. Sitting at the table, surrounded by my relatives and friends, I relished my good fortune.

The plane ride back to Canada was quiet and a bit melancholic for me. Despite the long flight, I couldn't rest. I kept thinking of all I had seen and experienced. My family was the biggest surprise. I didn't expect to be so welcomed by them or shown so much love where there had been none. I had a new spot in my heart for my mother. No longer kept in a dark pit in my mind, my mother became human. Time had probably been a good teacher to her, as it had been to me.

After all, it was a wonderful visit and I gave thanks.

The next few years didn't pass without challenges for Dan and me. I can't say they were all blissful, but our love for each other carried us through. For our first anniversary, we bought a Winnebago and drove across Canada to visit with Dan's family in Alberta and celebrate his grandfather's ninety-fourth birthday. The old gentleman made his way around in a wheelchair and on the night of his party, he grabbed my hand, looking pleased.

"Young lady," he said, "when I came from Germany seventy years ago, there wasn't a Trautman anywhere. Now look at this room. It makes a man proud."

Two years later he died, and Dan and I returned for the funeral. I'd never seen so many people honouring one man. The stories and poems told about his life brimmed with affection and admiration. I couldn't help but believe he had been a great person.

We bought a cottage two hours north of Newmarket. It was a tiny cottage, hardly big enough for the five of us. After a few months, Dan scouted the area for a bigger lot where he could build a bigger and better dwelling and soon enough, he found it.

I maintained a good relationship with my aunt and her family. Little Sabrina who wasn't so little anymore, beamed every time she saw me. Over time, she became a beloved little sister. My aunt would always be my saving angel and I never stopped loving and respecting her. Roger and Pedro and I never had much in common but I continued to love them both. As for my uncle, I couldn't avoid seeing him, however, only necessary words were ever exchanged between us. What he did to me was buried in silence, and for me, never forgotten and probably never forgiven. But they were my family, so I decided to let bygones be bygones and since I didn't see them often, I could live with my decision.

I was a happily married woman, and more than satisfied helping my husband raise his children. I wanted to be a good role model for them and worked hard to accomplish that. I never claimed to be perfect or to be any better than anyone else. I appreciate what I have and give thanks every day. My husband continued to be kind and good to me, and his children accepted me as a friend. I could not wish for anything more. In those early days, my relatives came to our house every once in a while, and I greeted them as a loving niece and cousin would.

As the years passed, old wounds were forgotten and I found myself softening more towards my mother, especially since seeing her on my honeymoon. I still sent her money when I could, never breaking the promise I made to her when she allowed me to come to Canada.

"I would like to bring your mother to visit Canada," Aunt Licinia told me casually one day after dinner, on one of their visits to our house and as we sat in the living room. "I miss my sister," she announced, sadly.

"Well then, bring her." I said, matter of fact.

"You wouldn't mind?" she asked hopeful. "I will keep her at my house and you can visit her anytime you want."

"Listen, Tia, go ahead and invite her. I will even help you pay for her plane fare."

"Are you serious? I have been thinking of this for quite a while but didn't know how you would react. I would never do anything to make you feel uncomfortable," my aunt said with conviction.

"It's okay, Tia, bring my mom over. Let me know the cost so I can chip in."

"Thank you, that takes such a heavy weight off my heart. You won't even have to see her if you don't want," she assured me.

"But I do, Tia. I do want to see her."

A month later my mother arrived in Canada and I invited the whole family to come to our house for the weekend. It was surreal to have my mother in Canada, in the safe haven I had escaped to. But it gave me a chance to see her relaxed and comfortable with her sister and with me as well, a different woman than the one I remembered. Gone was the cruel beauty who ignored me, beat me and berated me. Instead, I truly saw the person she was: insecure and uncertain, happy to be with family, intrigued by modern life in Canada. She stayed for a month and in that time, we had a few such visits and I discovered that I was growing fonder of my mother.

Finally, it was time for her to return to Portugal and as I said goodbye to her at the airport, sadness engulfed me for what could have been.

Chapter Twenty-Four

Up to the Boonies

Driving back from the cottage one Sunday afternoon, Dan stopped at a brand-new plaza near us where some units were empty.

"I just bought one of these units here, that one in the middle," he pointed. "See it?"

"I see it, what are you going to put there? Are you going to rent it out?"

"Let me ask you this," my husband said turning towards me in his truck. "If you had the chance to own your own business, what would you sell?"

"Well, let me see," I said pensive, rubbing my chin in concentration. "Food. People will always have to eat, right?" I said enthusiasticly.

"Well, think of what food you'd like to sell and that unit is yours to use."

"Really?" my eyes widened in surprise. "Ah, this is really exciting but that means I'll have to quit the health unit.

Dan started the truck and we headed for home, my head was full of possibilities.

"It'll be okay," I said on the way. "I think I can sell food. I have enough experience working with people. That's a deal, thank you," I said as a big smile spread across my face.

For the next few days, we searched for franchises we thought would make it in a small town like Newmarket. We came across a sandwich franchise we had never heard of, Subway. What kind of a name was that for a food chain? We looked at all the pictures of the menu offerings and everything looked so appetizing, I wanted to know more about it. Subway originated in the small town of Milford, Connecticut and its founder, Fred de Luca, started selling sandwiches in a small unit very much like our own. His mother sliced the meats in the back and he sold them at the front. His secret was the fresh baked bread. In order to advertise, he'd stand in a corner and hand out fliers to the public. He didn't have a car so when he went home on the subway, he handed fliers there, too. And thus, his sandwich shop became famous in the United States and would be famous throughout the world.

We researched other Canadian Subways so we could try the food, and the nearest location was at the Lakeshore Boulevard in Toronto. A long way to travel but by now, I was set on opening a Subway franchise.

At the little sandwich shop, we talked with the owner and tried some of his product. I had a seafood sub that, as I watched it be put together, made my mouth water and tasted even better. I was sold, I was going to be an entrepreneur. We got all the information and before I knew, our unit was being transformed and I was travelling to Milford for training.

We opened our store in July of 1988 and we were the tenth Subway shop in all of Canada. My last boss, the medical office of health for York Region was my first customer. I was nervous but I served him myself and when he finished his lunch, I gave him a tour of my shop. Dr. Slingerland was impressed.

"Very nice, Maria, you did well. Your shop is clean, your food was delicious and I will come back for more."

"Thank you, sir," I said as we shook hands. I had a fan.

The newness of Subway in our little community had people wondering what we were all about, they would come into the store a little curious but always left with a smile and the promise to come back. We had lineups to the door every single day and I trained my employees to always make eye contact with the last person in line and smile because more than likely, no matter how long the line was, they would stay.

To promote my store, I would go in early in the morning and do the prep for the day. I prepared large trays of my best and most expensive sandwiches and bring them to the police station, the fire department, the school offices in the area and of course, my friends at the health unit. They all tried my food and always came back for more. The only competition I had in the area was McDonald's and Mr. Sub. Fred de Luca, himself, told me that the best thing for a company to prosper was to have competition and to always open a sandwich shop near a McDonald's.

"They are established and kids love their food but how about the parents? Wouldn't they prefer a fresh salad with some of our delicious seafood on top or a tasty sub?"

A Mr. Sub franchise was just around the corner and was owned by a guy named Nick whom everyone knew. To my surprise, Nick came into my shop one day and ordered a steak sub and sat down to eat it. When he was done, the place was packed with a lineup to the door. Nick stood to leave but stopped and proclaimed, "Not a bad sandwich, but I still like Mr. Sub better."

"Sure, Nick," I called out from behind the counter. "Thank you for the compliment."

I operated my little sandwich shop successfully for the next ten years. During that time and after he had built us a new and much larger cottage, Dan insisted that we go north every Friday at noon. I hired a manager and was able to make my husband happy by arriving at the cottage every Friday by two in the afternoon. We enjoyed our weekends and so did the girls. We made new friends and built new relationships; the girls grew up.

As Louisa, Shelby and Claire got older, Shelby remained my greatest challenge. The teen years were difficult for her and for me but by the time she turned eighteen, she matured and so did our relationship.

Louisa studied Travel and Tourism in college. All she wanted to do when she grew up was to become the entertainment director of a big cruise ship.

Claire fell in love at sixteen and by seventeen she was married and had her first child, Lori. She eventually had two more children, Nicole and Michael.

In 1998, Dan talked of moving to the cottage permanently and living the simple life. He wanted to slow down, maybe even sell his company. I would have to sell the sandwich shop if we decided to make the big move and I was uncomfortable with the idea. Maybe Dan felt ready to settle down to a quieter life, but I had serious doubts that I was ready. I was only forty-five years old. The little sandwich shop had always been successful but it required me to be there at six a.m. every morning to prepare all the food for the day. Between the business and my home life, I was a very busy woman but if I moved to the country, what would I do? I would garden, I thought, and...and nothing.

"We could live at our cottage very comfortably," Dan said over dinner one night.

"You want us to live at the cottage?" I asked, surprised. "You're telling me we're going to live in the bush permanently?"

"I thought you liked our cottage," he said between bites.

"I love it, but I love it as a weekend home, not a permanent one." I tried to reason with him. "You like to go fishing and hunting with your friends for weeks at a time. That means I would have to live at the cottage by myself and that would be horrible. There's no one around during the offseason. It would just be me and the bears, the coyotes and God knows what else. Really, Dan, you can't be serious."

"You mean to tell me that if I want to retire, I'll have to buy another house?" he questioned.

I stood my ground. "I mean to tell you that if you want to retire in cottage country, we will have to live in town, where there are people."

The following week, a very grouchy Dan drove to the cottage for the weekend. He went into town to see his friend, Keith, who'd been an usher at our wedding and was a real estate agent in the area.

A week later he drove me back and I was taken to look at some of the most fabulous homes I had ever seen: One of them was three-stories and all of it, five thousand and four hundred square feet of pure elegance. The red brick dream house faced a lake and each bedroom had its own balcony. I adored the high ceilings and the large kitchen with the island in the middle. I was overwhelmed by it but I thought there was no way we'd be able to afford this fabulous house. At the same time, I wanted it. Low and behold and to our absolute shock, we got it. And at a price we could afford. The cottage would have to be put up for sale and as I had wished, we would live in the town proper.

The small place was not even a town, but a village with very few amenities. It was a bustling hub in the summer when all the cottagers would take up temporary residence and then the sidewalks roll up for the winter when those folks returned to their city lives. It made the village very quiet and somewhat lonesome, a desolate place to spend the winter.

The sandwich shop went up for sale immediately, ending my life as a business woman. I had done well and was pleased with how much I had learned but now, it was time to move to the next phase of my life.

Dan had previously operated a thriving business out of a building he owned in the older part of Newmarket, housing five electricians and three secretaries who worked for him. In the early nineties the town had a major growth phase. The local mall was renovated, new subdivisions sprouted where before there was only farmland, and the industrial sector also improved with the addition of larger and more modern commercial buildings. Never one who misses out on a good opportunity, Dan purchased one of these buildings and converted the old one into both a residence and a commercial building. The street level he rented to businesses and the second was renovated into three separate apartments. Dan kept one of them for our own use and rented the other two.

Dan wanted to retire but he never did. Now that he still had a place to live in Newmarket, he would spend the day at work during the week and only come home to me on the weekend. These were difficult times for me. I lived in a place where I didn't know anyone and no one would give me a job because the few that came up went to locals. Dan arrived home on Fridays, happy and ready to enjoy the weekend, but he would find me anxiously waiting for him, my welcoming smile barely reaching my eyes.

"What's the matter, sweetheart? You don't look very happy to see me." he would ask as he emptied a bag full of dirty clothes in the laundry room.

"Nothing," I always replied, afraid to disclose my true feelings and ruin his good mood. And then with tears threatening to spill, I would head back into the kitchen to prepare his dinner and camouflage my unhappiness by pretending all was well. I didn't want him to feel remorse or guilt about the decision of making me quit my job and uprooting me from a contented life in Newmarket.

My days were spent organizing the many rooms in our house and decorating them with the furniture and accessories from our former home and whatever I could find in the village.

On one of these days I came across a box inside one of the larger boxes I hadn't yet unpacked. I forgot about that familiar container that had travelled with me all the way from Portugal to Canada. Transported from one place to another, without me ever going through its contents. Inside that box, my many diaries that held stories of the toils I endured in my bleak childhood and when I first arrived in Canada. I began to journal in a diary shortly after I arrived at my mother's home and continued the practice when I joined my relatives in Canada.

On that day and many days following, it was easy for me in my present state of mind to reminisce about my arduous journey, as I read all the notebooks of yellowed, tear-stained paper. Through my handwritten texts, I relived those experiences in my life, and the warm stinging tears I had craftily suppressed, finally erupted with a fury that took immense effort to cease. Left in ruins, I fell asleep on the couch, my notebooks scattered around me, until the next day when I would resume my review and repeat the cycle.

I made a sincere effort to keep the joyful parts of my life's journey at the forefront of my mind. I decided long ago to bury the past and to live happily, but as I continued to read, the painful memories of my bizarre and turbulent childhood and young life finally collapsed and crumbled the careful wall I had erected around myself. The harrowing nightmares that plagued me for years returned.

I decided to move all the contents of the diaries into a folder on my computer so I would not have to look at them again, but the task proved to be more difficult that I initially thought. I relived my unsettled life day by day, typing about the monstrous things inflicted upon me. There were moments when I couldn't see the pages through the blur of tears. Emotional pain engulfed me, leaving my spirit exhausted. Yet, as I read and relived, I marvelled at the willpower and perseverance of my young self and admired the child who survived so much.

I had a home and a family I was proud of.

I decided to put self-pity on hold, I was safe.

I worked hard for my freedom and I would forever be humbled for my many blessings. I had always been embarrassed of my past and "not to tell" was ingrained in me. It took me a long time to be able to disclose most of what happened to me in this book but even as I write it down, my chest still feels tight and, as usual, I try not to dwell on it for too long. Over the years, I shared bits and pieces of my past with Dan but never got very specific about the horrendous things that were done to me. He has remained my rock, always loving and protecting me, no matter what he learned about my life.

Chapter Twenty-Five

The Search for The Beginning

Revisiting my past conjured up a father I knew nothing about. The lack of connection or any knowledge about him drilled a sad void deep within me. Although he had never been in my life, I wanted to know who he was. My desire was not driven by love but simply by curiosity. I needed to fill in the empty space. So, I decided to return to Portugal to try and find him. I knew Dan would support me but I wanted to know what he really thought about my leaving. I didn't know how long I'd be gone and I couldn't guarantee I'd come back with a happy ending.

One evening during dinner, I shared my idea with my husband. "I have been thinking about my father, lately, who he was or is. I'd like to know my roots."

"And what's stopping you?"

"Nothing, I suppose, except that it'll be expensive and I'm not sure it will be worth it."

"Tell me your plan," he said, smiling kindly.

"Well, first I have to get in touch with Tia Licinia and find out if she wants to go with me to Portugal. She knows where my father lived and I think I should start there. I need her help."

"Are you kidding me? Your aunt will love to go with you, of that I'm quite positive. Please continue."

"Then I'll have to book a flight, a car, and travel to Portugal without the faintest idea of what I'll find."

"I know you, my darling wife. You put something in your head and it won't leave you until you do something about it. Go. Go on your quest and find your roots so you can relax and live your life. You have my blessing."

"I knew you would say that, thank you. It's just that if I don't do it now, while I can, I will wonder forever," I said.

He covered my hand with his. "Take your time and do your search, Maria, I will miss you but I want you to be happy and have no regrets."

My Tia Licinia lived alone. Her children had their own families, and my uncle had left her for one of her best friends. When I went to see her and told her about my plan, she wasn't sure about finding my roots but she did say she would be happy to accompany me to Portugal. I wrote to my mother to tell her we were coming and the reason why. She was going to be shocked at the news but it was my quest, after all.

I have read about and seen the movies where people want to find their biological parents and I know people who would say, "So what? Why would you want to find him after all these years?" But a voice within was telling me, "Go, before it's too late."

In our early years at the cottage, we met many wonderful people. Tulia was one person whom I loved at first sight. She was also Portuguese so we had a lot in common. We'd spend weekends getting together, eating together and talking for hours by the bonfire. We truly bonded. She lived in Toronto and I lived two hours north of there so we made a pact. On my birthday and then again on her birthday, I would visit her in Toronto for the weekend and we would go shopping and out for dinner. The reason I went to Toronto both times is because she lived near many Portuguese shops where I could buy and bring home all sorts of Portuguese delicacies not available in our town. This became a tradition and as a result, we became the best of friends. I went to visit her just before I left to go back to Portugal.

After we had a delicious dinner in one of our favourite restaurants, she said to me, "That's quite an adventure, Maria, I wish you the best. Hey, you know I have a condo in Caldas. You know that it's midway between Lisbon and your village. Why don't you and your aunt stay there? Free of charge, my friend."

My aunt and I arrived in Portugal in the summer of 2003.

As soon as we landed, I rented a car and drove towards the airport exit. The chaos of a bustling city overwhelmed me. After a night of sitting on a plane without sleep, I was exhausted. My aunt was not a navigator nor did she drive, so it looked very confusing to her as well. I got to a roundabout that took up a whole city square and reminded me of a giant octopus, its tentacles writhing in several directions. I tried to find the street that would take me out of the busy city but everything was a blur.

"You've gone around three times," my aunt piped up. "People will think you're crazy. Are you turning somewhere?"

"I know Tia, give me a moment, I'm looking." I said, a bit irritated.

"Just exit the roundabout anywhere, we'll figure it out then."

I did and was shocked when I realized I was going in the right direction. "Thank you," I whispered.

It was early morning in Lisbon and crowds of pedestrians could be seen walking along the pavement outside the shops or trying to cross the streets. I knew I had to drive through the city in order to get to my mother on the other side of the Tagus river. But from deep within the city, all I could see were the towers and suspension cables of the bridge and had no idea where the bridge connected with the city.

After many wrong turns and one in particular where I got stopped by the police because it was an illegal left-hand turn, I found the bridge and headed to my mother's home. By the time I finally got out of the car and in spite of it being early morning, I had a strong desire to have a good stiff drink.

The first person I saw was my stepfather who had just returned from the bakery and was holding a plastic bag with several small breads. After the initial greeting, the little man looked at me and said, "Put on a little weight, didn't you?" and smiled merrily, accentuating the two dimples in the middle of both his cheeks.

I was about to say, "I can always take the weight off but you're ugly, what are you going to do about that?" but ended up changing my mind. Made me smile just thinking about it though. He grabbed both our suitcases and we headed to their little dwelling.

As we walked, I could hear the sound of the waves breaking on the beach nearby and before long, the majestic expansion of the Atlantic Ocean was before us. I stopped and closed my eyes, taking a deep breath of the sea air, feeling some of the tension that had been building in me ebb away.

Seventeen years had passed since I had last come to Portugal for my honeymoon but the feeling of familiarity never faded, Portugal was such a beautiful country. My mother welcomed us and I was glad to see her again. She was thinner and more fragile and, as she came closer, she peered at me through the much thicker lenses in her glasses. Her eyes looked enormous. Her hair had little grey in it but her face looked gaunt and tired, although she was only seventy-two years old. She approached me with open arms and I walked into her embrace.

"So good to see you, my daughter," she said as she hugged me. In my arms, my mother felt small and fragile and I found myself gently hugging her back.

"Good to see you as well, Mom. I hope you are ready to travel to Granja with Tia and me, tomorrow." I said cheerfully.

"Never liked the place and never will. Just a dirty old village with dirty old people," she said bitterly.

"Please don't say that, Mom. Granja was my home where I lived with Grandma and Grandpa and, to me, it holds beautiful memories," I said. "I have come here to find out about my father. I need to know where my roots are and I need your help."

The welcoming look was replaced with one of censure. "Why bother? Everyone is dead and you're wasting your time," she said.

"I travelled all the way here from Canada for this and I'm going to complete my mission. I'm sure there has to be someone in my father's village who can tell me something. You are welcome to come with Tia and me or you can stay here."

My mother narrowed her eyes behind their thick lenses and then shook her head, annoyed. "I would like to go with you but I'm telling you it's a waste of time, everyone is dead."

"And how do you know that? Have you been to Joao Durao lately?" I snapped, a bit annoyed.

"Of course not, nor would I want to, but it's been too long, you won't find anyone."

"Mother, I don't want to hear another word about this. I am here to find out who my father was. Since you never gave me much information, I have to go and find out for myself." I didn't want to be mean but the time for her to tell me what to do had long passed. She didn't bother to reply, just turned around and headed to the little kitchen where my stepfather was preparing a meal.

I didn't get much sleep that night, either. I shared the bed with my aunt and although she had no problem falling asleep, unrest seized me as I lay awake with my thoughts. Once in a while I heard what sounded like mice somewhere within the walls and that didn't help.

After a restless night, I got up early. I had no idea what time it was and it was too dark to read my watch so I made my way outside. I could barely see the two chairs outside the door and sat on one of them. The air was chilly and I was glad I had set a sweater by my bed before I went to sleep. I wrapped it around me and looked out to sea. Even though I couldn't see them the waves lapped against the sand like a lullaby and the dark water was tinged with soft shades of yellow and orange. The sun would soon be up and so would everyone inside. I was happy for these few moments alone to organize my thoughts.

My mother may have been right to be bitter at me wanting to find my father and she was probably correct in her assumption that he may already be dead. Also, if I found my father or his wife, or any of his family, was I prepared for the disdain, the spurning of me from their front door, just as they had spurned my mother when they found out she was with child?

Everyone in the village had known there was no one in my mother's life. No one, except for her Patrao—my father, Afonso, who raped my mother, a defenseless and young village girl, without any thought about future consequences, just because he could. A teacher of children, he was not exactly ignorant of the ramifications of such a heinous act. Yet he failed to provide his bastard with the basic necessities of life or even acknowledge her existence. As far as I was concerned, the man could burn in hell for eternity. But I still wanted to know who the pervert had been. This was my quest.

Many times, when I was being abused, I prayed that I wouldn't get pregnant so history would not repeat itself. I shiver with repulsion every time I think of Mr. Santos or my uncle having their way with me. But, what could I have done? Nothing. I was alone in my torment. What control do you have when someone threatens your very life? What control do you have when the imbecile over you is four times your size?

What is it with reckless older men who take advantage of an innocent child or frightened girl? They hold nothing in their hearts but perversion, selfishness, ego and lack of respect for another human being.

The sun was about to break the horizon and I thought it best to stop my reverie and observe Mother Nature at her best. The sky and the ocean waters were suddenly ignited with fiery shades of red, orange and yellow, as the sun was about to make its grand entrance. Soon, the first people would arrive at the beach to set up their tents in their favourite spots so that later they could take refuge from the heat of the day.

"There you are," came a sleepy voice behind me. "How long have you been out here?" my aunt asked.

"It was hot in bed and I couldn't sleep. We'll leave as soon as everyone is up."

"They are both up now. I saw your stepfather help your mother get dressed."

The bags were packed and I stood waiting for my mother and aunt to get in the car when my stepfather came to check on his wife. "Do you have your comfortable shoes packed? You can't wander all over the country in those heels, let me see them."

"Stop worrying about me," she hissed.

"Do you have enough money? Here, take some more," he said as he took some bills out of his wallet. He then turned to me.

"She's not good in the head, you know. I always have to keep my eye on her because half the time she doesn't even know what day it is." He turned to my mother again. "Where's your medication? Let me see it."

After what seemed an eternity getting my mother organized, we finally got settled into the car and on the road.

Driving north was pure pleasure. Once I left the madness of the city and merged onto highway A1, I relaxed and took in the amazing landscapes of the countryside. Large clusters of trees offered canopies of shade to various groups of animals. I spotted goats and sheep, horses and cattle, some enjoying the break from the sun while others roamed the green fields. At some point I veered off at a break on the narrow highway and onto what I thought was still the right road, only to end up going up a mountain. There was no chance of turning around anywhere because the road was so narrow so I continued climbing, wondering what I would find on my way.

We arrived at a small clearing at the top of the mountain, and the road ended here. After reading a sign that advertised a restaurant, I didn't need any encouragement to stop so we could enjoy some lunch. Everyone agreed.

From that high up, the landscape was breathtaking. A gentle breeze caressed the long grasses on the side of the hills and the leaves on the trees, making them dance in the sunshine. Far below, vein-like waterways meandered through lush green valleys. I noticed a small winding road on the opposite side we came up on and thought that may be the way back down but first, we would enjoy a country meal.

While we waited for the food, I took out my maps and spread them on the table for a quick review. All the larger villages were outlined, Vila Franca das Naves, Pinhel, Trancoso and others I had heard of, but the ones I was looking for were nowhere on the map. I hoped the memories of my two travelling partners were clear enough to guide me there.

We stopped in Villa Franca das Naves where I booked two rooms at one of the new hotels that had not been there when I lived in Granja. We had a meal and a good night's sleep and the next morning after breakfast, we continued our journey. We travelled on the dusty roads I remembered so well and I looked for the mimosa trees but without blooms, they were just clusters of unrecognizable trees to me. At first, we travelled the road leading to Granja but then we had to veer off to another road my aunt recognized as the one leading to Joao Durao, the village my father lived in until I was born. We passed rustic signs nailed to tree trunks announcing the name of the villages and other times the name was just scribbled on a large rock, but the one we were looking for was nowhere to be seen. After a while, I began to wonder if maybe the sign fell to the ground but then again, perhaps we were lost. A bit farther along, my aunt spotted a boulder with some letters barely visible due to the high grasses but there was no doubt that the name on the rock with an arrow pointing the way we were travelling was Joao Durao.

When we entered the village, it seemed abandoned. Farther along the road we spotted a flock of chickens pecking the earth beside one of the houses, oblivious to the car that had just driven past them. I also noticed laundry drying on an old clothesline but where were the people? Perhaps they were all in the fields, working.

Finally, I saw an old man walking with the aid of a cane and stopped the car. He also stopped to peer curiously at us and when I got out, he lifted his cane in greeting. He had only two teeth in his head one on top, another on the bottom. The man's rheumy eyes were a vacant stare and when I asked about my father's family, he shook his head and remained silent. I knew I would get nothing from him so I got back in the car and kept driving.

A short distance later my aunt sat up straight. "Stop the car. Stop the car!" she shouted. "Angelina, isn't that the house?"

I stopped and looked at where she was pointing, seeing what must have once been a grand house.

The outer block stone shell remained but the windows no longer held any glass. The stone wall surrounding the yard had deteriorated almost to the ground and a rusty gate hung awkwardly from its top hinges.

We sat in the car for a moment in wordless silence, wondering what to do. I caught a movement in the rear-view mirror and saw an old woman walking towards us. Encouraged by any sign of life, I stepped out of the car again and smiled at her.

"Excuse me, but do you know anyone who's related to the people who lived here?" I asked, gesturing towards the house.

She shook her head. "No, the people who lived there left for Brazil a long time ago."

"I know they did, but are there any relatives in this village?" I asked, feeling hopeless.

"No, there aren't," she said, waving her hand at the house. "The whole family left."

I thanked her and turned back towards the car, feeling very disappointed. Was this the end of my search? I had no idea where to go from there and I feared if I was lucky enough to find another person here, their answer would probably be the same. This woman was ancient, she had probably lived here all her life. If she didn't know, I doubted anyone else would. Perhaps my mother was right, maybe everyone *was* dead. I got back in the car and was relieved when no one said a word.

I drove with no direction. I didn't know the way out of the village nor did I care, I just drove, becoming increasingly despondent over my failing attempt to find anything about my father.

The number of houses was becoming scarcer and I presumed I was leaving Joao Durao behind when I saw a woman working in a field, piling what appeared to be vegetables into two bags strapped to an old donkey.

I got out of the car and waved to the woman. In response, she left the animal and walked towards the road. It took her a little while to get to me, her legs seeming stiff and arthritic.

"Good afternoon," I said. "I'm looking for someone who may remember a man who was a teacher in this village fifty years ago. He was my father, and his name was Afonso. Can you help me?"

The old woman brought a wrinkled hand to her face in thought. She shook her head. "Fifty years ago? I was just a girl then. I'm sorry, but I can't remember anyone with that name," she said, a look of compassion clearly expressed on her face. I started to thank her when the woman suddenly cried, "Wait, Senhor Franco is just in the next field and he may be able to help you, come with me."

She started walking away and I followed her to the edge of the road then stopped when I spotted a man in a field below. He was shovelling hay into a cart behind a tractor but came to a halt when he saw the old woman coming towards him. They talked for a few moments and there was a lot of gesturing in my direction, then he started walking towards the road. As he drew closer and fixed his gaze upon me, his smile broadened. This was the most excitement we'd seen all day and my palms dampened with anticipation.

"You know, you look like him," he said, his mouth and eyes smiling merrily. He reached out and shook my hand. "I remember Eduardo Afonso."

Eduardo Afonso, that was my father's name. My knees weakened and I felt overwhelmed by emotion but Franco didn't seem to notice, he just kept talking.

"His wife was also a teacher and I had the misfortune of being in her class. That woman was so cruel, she beat me within an inch of my life once for something I didn't even do."

"Senhor Franco," I interrupted gently. I feared he might never stop and I needed information. "I am not here to make any claims of my father or his family, I just want to know about my roots. I never even knew his full name until now. I just need to ask you a few questions."

He tilted his head and regarded me sadly as if he realized there must have been a tragedy behind what I was saying. He then smiled compassionately and nodded, encouraging me to tell my story. So, I did.

I stood on that dusty road and told my story to a stranger. The old woman stood beside us while my mother and aunt still sat in the car.

When I finished talking, Senhor Franco nodded slowly. "You need to talk with his niece, Natalia. She lives in Freixedas, the next village. She will be able to give you all the information you need."

"Would you be able to come with me and introduce me to her?" I asked. "I will drive you back to your field afterwards."

He stood taller, excitement showing on his face. "Yes, yes," he said. "Let's go."

After we'd joined the others in the car, I introduced him to my aunt and mother, then drove towards Freixedas. My head was in turmoil, my heart pounding.

My father. I was finally going to find out about my father.

Chapter Twenty-Six

A Door Opens

When we arrived at Freixedas, Franco guided me through the narrow roads until we reached a two-story house on a street corner. The door on the first floor was open and as my eyes focused on the dark interior, I could see a form moving about. It seemed to be a stable of some kind which would've been the basement of the house. Franco got out of the car and went inside, returning after a few moments accompanied by a woman. I found myself face to face with my father's niece, my first cousin, Natalia.

She regarded me with apprehension as I smiled and extended my hand.

"It's a pleasure to meet you," I said as we shook hands. "My name is Maria de Lourdes Almeida Trautman, and I think you're my cousin. My mother used to work for your uncle, my father.

Natalia was silent and her expression unreadable.

"Before you say anything, I want you to know that I'm not here to make any claims or impose on anyone, I simply want to know about my father. I came all the way from Canada to discover who he was. Can you help me?"

The woman's expression relaxed. "You know," she said, "I remember when I was eleven, maybe twelve, my father came home one day and said to my mother, "Angelina is with child.""

I caught my breath, mesmerized.

Natalia smiled, seeing my reaction. "My mother asked him how he knew that, and he told her he'd seen Angelina going to the well to get water. He said that when she lifted the water jar out of the well, she did so with some effort. "She had to bend her legs and squat, as if she were protecting her belly," my father said.

My mother protecting me? What an alien concept.

I wondered if I should go out to the car and invite my aunt and my mother to come and join the conversation but then I decided not to, this was my moment.

"I never thought of that incident again until now," she mused. "After your mother left, we knew she had a baby, but we didn't know if it was a boy or a girl." She smiled warmly at me. "But come in, come into my house and we can talk some more."

Natalia led the way and I followed her, Senhor Franco not far behind me. We walked around the house until we came to the front entrance, then climbed a flight of stairs to the second floor. Senhor Franco came with us and Natalia didn't seem to mind. I had the feeling this event was very exciting for him as well and he didn't want to miss any of it.

"Please sit down," my cousin said, gesturing towards an elegant sofa draped with some sort of lace. The sitting room was well furnished, with plenty of china in the cabinet and beautiful paintings and expensive-looking decorative objects on the walls and mantel.

"Would you like something to eat or drink?" Natalia asked.

"No, thank you," I replied, settling on the sofa. "Please tell me, cousin, is my father still alive? Is he still in Brazil?"

Natalia tilted her head to one side and sighed, looking regretful. "No, I'm sorry, he died years ago. His family is still there though. Did you know you have a brother and a sister?"

It was too late, after all. I felt a pang of sorrow for this father of mine, the man I never knew and now I never would. At least he'd left bits and pieces of him behind.

"I knew he had a wife and children," I replied to my cousin's question. "But I never knew their names or how old they were. Can you tell me about them?"

She sat on the sofa beside me, looking pleased that she could help.

"My uncle Eduardo and his wife, Matilda, left for Brazil when their daughter, Claudia, was eleven and Marco, your brother, was a couple of years younger. I remember my uncle loved to ride his motorcycle and I believe it was because of that motorcycle that he went deaf and had to quit his job as a teacher.

"A few years after that they left for Brazil and we heard he developed cancer of the larynx and died of complications. I couldn't really tell you when that happened, it seems like such a long time ago," she paused, lost in thought and then, her face brightened.

"I think I have a picture of my uncle; would you like it?"

This was more wonderful than I'd imagined. Tears filled my eyes. "Oh yes, please."

Natalia rose and left the room for a few minutes. When she returned, she handed me two tiny pictures of my father as if they were prized possessions. I looked at the black and white images of a handsome man, perhaps in his late twenties and wearing an army uniform. I wondered how this man could've willingly ignore the existence of his flesh and blood. How could this wholesome-looking human have been the cause of so much pain?

This was my father, the phantom man I had wondered about all my life. Of course, when I was born, he was much older, married with children and probably a lot surer of himself and his power. The next photo was of him as well but older. Natalia couldn't tell me what his age was then and I couldn't guess.

"God love and forgive him," I said softly, studying the photographs. I looked back up at Natalia. "May I borrow them so I can make copies? I will return them to you."

"They're yours. No need to return them. I am just happy to have been helpful. Tell me, dear." My cousin leaned forward. "Why don't you get in touch with your brother and sister?"

The question hit me by surprise.

"I would love to but as I said before, I don't want to impose on anyone. This happened such a long time ago and I don't want to disrupt their lives by making them relive a sad period."

"Oh, I don't know," she said thoughtfully. "I bet they would like to hear from you. Why don't I get you their address?"

"If you're sure it's no trouble," I said.

"Oh no, no, no trouble at all. Wait here while I phone my sister, she's the one who communicates with everyone in Brazil."

I waited with Senhor Franco who sat motionless, taking everything in and not saying a word. A few seconds later we heard Natalia on the phone. I couldn't hear the person at the other end, but I heard Natalia's reply.

"No, she is not going to bother them and she wants nothing from them, she just wants to write to her siblings and tell them who she is."

That told me her sister had thought what I'd feared, that I was there to disrupt their lives, maybe stake a claim. When Natalia returned and handed me the address, I thanked her but assured her I probably wouldn't be using it.

"I'll give you my information," I said. "If you talk with them and they want to know me, please give it to them."

The meeting was over. I hugged my cousin and thanked her for everything, all the information, the photo of my father, and for getting my siblings' address for me. Her hug was strong and sincere and as we drove away, she stood outside her house and waved.

I brought Senhor Franco back to his field and as I got out of the car to say goodbye, I reached into my pocket and pulled out a twenty euro note.

"This is to buy a beer on me," I said, extending my hand. "I want to thank you for all you've done."

"Please," he replied, waving his hand in dismissal of the money. "Don't insult me by paying me for what I did. It was my pleasure. I'm glad I was able to help you find what you were looking for."

"I don't mean any insult," I assured him, putting the money back in my pocket. "I just wanted you to know how much I appreciate your help."

He hooked both thumbs in the waistband of his trousers and his face softened with a wistful smile. "You know, at one time, I was one of the most prominent people in this village. I have travelled the world but I always end up back here because this is home."

I said goodbye and as I shook his hand, he wished me a safe trip home.

I noticed the old woman still in her field. The donkey dozed in the shade of a large chestnut tree and the woman was bent over, hoe in hand and turning the soil. When she saw me walking towards her, she straightened and smiled, wiping the sweat off her brow with the back of her hand. I extended my hand to thank her and then placed the twenty euros in her hand. Her face was so wrinkled—most likely due to the excessive exposure to the elements—that it looked like parchment paper, heavily etched with hieroglyphics. Her eyes however, beamed with kindness and wisdom.

"Thank you so much for all your help," I said.

I told her Franco had introduced me to my cousin and I was happy with the information I got. Her weathered face broke into a smile. "You are very welcome, my dear."

She reminded me of my own grandmother. It seems all the older women dressed the same way in that part of the world. Tradition dictates if there is a death in the family, especially if it is a husband or a son, the woman must wear black for the rest of her natural life.

I waved goodbye and walked back to the car where my mother and aunt were waiting for me. As I drove back down the dusty road, I handed my father's picture to my mother. She was sitting quietly in the back seat.

"Is this him, Mom?" I asked.

"Yes," came the faint reply.

"His name is Eduardo Afonso, and he is dead," I told her. "His wife is still alive though, and I have a sister and a brother in Brazil. My cousin suggested I write to them."

She thought about that. "Well," she said, "I thought he might be dead by now. He would be a very old man if he wasn't. Why would you want to write to those people anyway? It's been so long, they wouldn't remember you even if they had met you."

"Because those people as you put it, Mother, are my family." I snapped, exasperated. "I may not ever write to them, but it's nice to finally discover a little about where I came from. Especially learning my father's name."

I was close to tears but I didn't want to cry. I didn't say any more, just concentrated on driving. After a long silence, my mother's voice came from the back seat, sounding tired.

"Before you were born, he wanted me to have an abortion. I was too scared so I refused. Just think," she said, using a tone that made me look in the rear-view mirror. "If it had been up to him, we wouldn't even be having this conversation."

My head buzzed with confusion and more questions, though I was afraid to ask them. According to my mother, it had been my father who hadn't wanted me. He'd wanted me out of the way. But my mother ... she couldn't have wanted me either, could she?

And yet, here I sat.

Why had she kept me? Had they been in love after all? Was I a love child? Or had he simply taken advantage of a servant because he could?

I lived all my life presuming my mother had been raped, that my father was wealthy and had given her nothing but grief. But now I was left wondering. Was I the result of love or lust? I would never know for sure but if I thought of what happened to me, love was not the answer.

I tried to concentrate on my driving. From the corner of my eye I noticed my aunt looking at me as I brushed a tear off my cheek. I had to stop torturing myself with doubts. What did it all matter now? I was still pleased that I had at least discovered the full name of the man who had participated in giving me life, which, in spite of a miserable beginning, had turned out to be full and good. After this day, my father would become a flesh-and-blood man to me, no longer a vague phantom.

The trip back to Villa Franca das Naves was short and we were quiet most of the way. Once in a while my aunt spotted a fig tree on the side of the road and begged me to stop. She and I got out, but my mother stayed in the car. When we offered her some figs, she silently declined with a shake of her head. It seemed she was still brooding over my outburst, or perhaps she was only deep in her own thoughts.

We returned to Lisbon the next day. I left my mother with my stepfather, then headed to Caldas with my aunt, promising to go to dinner with the family before we returned to Canada.

Because my aunt and I were staying at Tulia's house which was some distance away from Lisbon, I hadn't seen Ana or Paulo.

My aunt and I visited all the tourist attractions around Caldas and toured Lisbon, too. On our last day, I took the whole family out to dinner as promised.

Chapter Twenty-Seven

A Family Found

I was relieved to return to familiar Canadian surroundings and see my husband again. It felt good to be home.

Through my journey I had accomplished a lifetime goal. Though I was sorry to have never met my father, I was satisfied with the outcome. I doubted I would ever hear from Natalia again but I still had my father's pictures, which I enlarged and sent her copies. I felt complete and no longer restless, the ache in my heart had melted away.

Fate, however, threw another curve ball across my path. Two weeks after I arrived home from Portugal, I received a letter in the mail from a woman in Toronto, claiming to be my cousin. I stood stock still in the middle of the post office as I read the letter.

"My name is Anabela Afonso Esteves, your cousin. I live in Toronto with my husband Steve and my daughter Gabriela," she wrote. "My sister, Inez, also lives in Toronto with her husband Joao and her son John. We would like to meet you sometime. If you would like to meet us, here is my address and phone number."

My face must have gone pale, because the clerk asked me if I was all right. I nodded, speechless, unable to believe my eyes. This letter carried such good news. Here was more family I hadn't known about. When I got home, I called my newly discovered cousin, Anabela, and we talked for a very long time. She invited me to visit her in Toronto, and we set a date for a week later.

I pulled up in front of my cousin's house, my palms damp with nervous sweat. I sat a moment in my car, trying to work up my nerve. Then the door swung open on the other side of the street and I saw Anabela, her husband Steve, and her sister Inez, walking towards me. The smiles on all their faces brought one to my own, dispelling any of my reservations. We all hugged and kissed on both cheeks, then Anabela took my hand and guided me into her house. Once inside, I noticed a large table covered with all sorts of Portuguese delicacies, and I couldn't help feeling amazed at how much trouble they'd gone to. I hadn't seen so much food in a very long time. These were Portuguese folks all right.

The conversation was easy and as I had expected, they wanted to know all about me. I spoke for a while, not holding back. They never interrupted me, not even when a tear slid down my cheek. I felt Anabela's hand cover mine and give an encouraging squeeze, so I continued with my tale. When I was done, the room was quiet for a moment but it was a comfortable silence. I felt totally at ease with my new cousins.

"Now," I said. "I want to know how you learned about me."

Anabela smiled. "We have a house in Porto," she began. "Every year for the past twenty years, we've spent three months in Portugal, we love it there. Steve and I enjoy visiting Lisbon, shopping and travelling around. Even though we go there a lot, I hadn't been to the village since I'd left as a young girl. This year I felt something different. It was as if something was telling me I must visit, I had to go back. I occasionally correspond with some of our relatives so I knew Natalia was still there. She and I had never been close so I'd had no reason to visit but now, I felt compelled to speak with her. When I got there, the first thing she said was that we had another cousin in Canada."

We all grinned at each other, mutually pleased to be learning so much about our family.

"I asked where this cousin was in Canada and I was both thrilled and surprised when she said Toronto."

Although I didn't live in Toronto at the time, whenever I am outside Canada and people ask me where I'm from, I always chose a central place they may have heard of.

"How could Inez and I have been living there all this time and never known?" She shook her head. "Natalia explained that it was Tio Eduardo's daughter, Lourdes. She told me that you had come to see her."

I nodded. "It was wonderful. I never thought I'd find out so much that day."

"Well, at first I thought Natalia was insane," Anabela continued. "She's getting older and I thought she was probably imagining things but when she told me the whole story, I understood."

"You know what is really strange?" I asked. "Twenty-five years ago, I worked at the bank just around the corner from your house. If only I had known."

"Me, too," she replied. "Twenty-five years ago, Inez was still in Portugal and I was here alone, with no family. Just Steve and me.

We talked through the whole afternoon and she finally gave me a tour of her house and yard, proudly pointing out her cherry and apple trees. We talked as if we had known each other all our lives and I knew they would become a dear part of my life.

"Why don't you write to your sister and brother in Brazil? I'm sure they would love to know they have a half-sister." Anabela asked.

"I don't know," I said. "I would like to know them but I don't want to disrupt their lives. I don't want to bring back any bad memories and besides, I don't even know if they've been told about me."

"I barely remember your sister and brother," she said. "We used to play together when we were children, but then they left and I never saw them again after that. But after meeting you today, I'm sure they would love to know you."

"I agree," Inez said. "I talk with your sister and brother on the phone once in a while, and they're very nice people."

"I don't know," I said with a shrug. I still felt hesitant at intruding on my half-siblings' lives. "We'll see."

Anabela wanted me to stay the night but I decided to go home. I did, however, invite all of them to come to our home and meet Dan.

After that day, I kept in touch with Anabela and Inez by phone. Every time we talked, she asked me if I had written to my half-sister and half-brother and I always gave the same answer. I hadn't summoned the courage to do it yet. I had lived without them all my life and now I feared they might reject me. At this point, I thought I'd rather live with uncertainty than with rejection. My father had rejected me and they were his family. Maybe I just wasn't meant to know them.

My new-found relatives visited us for a weekend in August, about a year after I met Natalia. It was wonderful seeing all of them together. They were such pleasant people to be with and I considered myself blessed for having them in my life. Dan liked them, too.

He seemed to have a lot in common with the men, since they hung around together all weekend, playing horseshoes, going for boat rides, and talking easily on the porch. The girls and I were also busy, talking, cooking, and getting to know each other. In the evenings we all came together and played cards.

Before they left on Sunday, Anabela asked me again to write to my siblings. I finally agreed.

I decided to write to my half-sister first, wondering what sort of reception my letter might get. I sat at my desk and printed a recent photo of myself and included it with my letter.

> Dear Claudia,
> My name is Maria de Lourdes Almeida Trautman, and I am your half-sister. I was born in 1953, my mother was your housekeeper and your father was my father as well. I just learned about you through our cousin Natalia in Freixedas. I also met our cousins

Anabela and Inez here in Canada, and

they talked me into writing to you.

I would love to know you but if

you don't want to know me, I will

understand. Just know that I am here.

Lourdes

I sent her my address and phone number, not expecting to hear from her, but two weeks later my phone rang. I could hardly contain myself when I heard my half-sister's voice at the other end.

"My God, I am so happy to hear your voice." Claudia exclaimed. "When I received your letter, I was in shock. I didn't even know I had a sister. My mother is eighty-nine and doesn't hear well anymore but I read her your letter and she confirmed what you said. You are my half-sister. Oh, I am so glad you decided to write to me."

"It took me a long time," I admitted. "But I finally realized I had to let you know I existed."

"Thank you for sending a photograph. You are very pretty," she said. "I tried to see the family resemblance and I think you look more like our brother, Marco, than me. I look like my mom."

I asked her about our father and she told me everything Natalia had said, only she had dates to go with everything.

"Our father, Eduardo Afonso, was born in 1912. He died in 1979 of cancer complications," she said. "Our family came to Brazil in 1953 to join our uncle and his family. Our father's brother promised him he could make a good living working here, but that didn't happen. Since father was deaf, it was difficult for him to find work."

And he couldn't go back to the village because I was there, I thought.

"Eventually, he resorted to growing his own vegetables and selling them at the local market, in order to keep food on our table. But we had some good times, too. He loved his family and was a good, gentle man. We all miss him very much."

I wished I could have known my father while he was alive so I could kick his ass. But I kept that thought to myself.

Claudia continued. "His eyes were the colour of honey and when he smiled, it was almost as if the sun radiated from them. Since he was deaf, he rarely spoke out loud. Any time he had to communicate with anyone, it was either through body language or else he used his little pad of paper and pen. Everyone understood him and everyone liked him."

Well, it seems he got what was coming to him, I thought.

After that conversation, many more followed. Anabela and Inez were also talking with my half-sister and I enjoyed the fascinating concept of the whole family communicating. I asked Claudia if she would consider visiting Canada but she wasn't too receptive to the idea, so I began to think about visiting Brazil.

I told Dan about my plan and he was all for it.

"I have lots of Air Miles points," he said. "You could probably go to Brazil and back, first class."

One day in October I was talking with Claudia, and she mentioned that Marco's birthday was coming up on the eighth of November. I had not yet spoken with my half-brother.

"Why don't you surprise him on his birthday?" my half-sister suggested. "He would love to hear from you."

I promised her I would do that, then mentioned I was going to visit them in Brazil.

She sounded excited. "When are you planning on coming?"

"Sometime in the new year."

"Wonderful!" she exclaimed.

On November eighth, I swallowed my nervousness and phoned my half-brother, Marco. I planned to sing Happy Birthday to him in Portuguese but when he answered the phone, I was so tongue-tied I could barely say hello. He put me at ease immediately by telling me how happy they were that I had found them, and how he hoped we could all let bygones be bygones.

"We don't know the circumstances, let's just be happy we found each other." he said.

Early in the new year, Dan took me to the airport and wished me luck, knowing how nervous I was to be meeting people I had never seen before. He talked me through hours of doubts leading up to this, reassuring me, understanding my fears that they might not readily accept me into their lives. But I had to at least try. I spent my entire life wondering where I had come from, never having many answers. I'd also always believed in destiny. Everything happens for a reason.

I went to Brazil with an open mind, telling myself that if they didn't like me, I would simply stay at a hotel for the remainder of my trip and have a wonderful time by myself.

It was a long flight to Sao Paulo and from there, I flew to Rio de Janeiro. I had sent my itinerary to my half-sister and hoped someone would be waiting for me.

As I pushed my cart in the reception area, I looked around but didn't recognize any of the faces I saw. My sister had sent me a photo of all of them with other relatives but all the faces I had memorized were not in the crowded room. I turned at the sound of commotion behind me and saw a group of people walking quickly, peering around as if they didn't know exactly what they were looking for. Then a man approached and looked right into my eyes.

"Lourdes? Is that you?"

"Yes," I answered, and ran into the open arms of my half-sister's husband. The next thing I knew, my half-brother Marco was behind him holding the biggest bouquet of red roses I had ever seen.

Then I was hugging him, Claudia, Marco's wife Julia, and their beautiful daughter, Liliana. When I hugged my half-sister, it felt like the most natural thing I had ever done, as if I had known her all my life. The same with my brother and his family. Everyone was friendly and accepting, happy to meet me.

When we arrived at Claudia's house, the first person I saw was Dona Matilda, my father's wife. I walked up to her and she took my hands in hers and kissed both my cheeks. At that moment, I didn't want to think how this woman had treated my mother in the past, she was an old woman now and I treated her with respect. She sensed that.

It seemed as if the news that I was coming had spread because there were people who did not come to greet me but simply satisfied their curiosity by staring at me. Some of them looked familiar, perhaps from the photograph. Claudia's two daughters, Ligia and Monica, also came out to greet me. They were polite but reserved.

When we went into my sister's house, the crowd I had not been introduced to dispersed, their curiosity satisfied.

During the week I spent there, I saw some of the gawkers occasionally but mostly they just ignored me. It was okay. I didn't have any inferiority complexes, so I just dealt with it and ignored them in turn.

We spent the rest of the first day and well into the night asking and answering questions.

Smiles were plenty and the atmosphere comfortable. I was staying at my sister's house so when my brother and his wife and the beautiful Liliana left, I was addressed as aunt and sister when they said goodnight.

I woke up early the next morning and the house was quiet. I made my way to the living room and noticed Dona Matilda seated on the sofa. She didn't hear me come into the room so I just sat quietly beside her.

She smiled gently and turned to me. "Your mother, where does she live?"

"She lives in Lisbon," I replied.

"Does she have other children?"

"Yes, a boy and a girl."

"I wish her all the happiness," she said.

"Thank you."

We sat in silence for a few seconds, then she turned to me again and said, "Sometimes in life, things happen that we have no control over, don't they? And then here we are, decades later, wondering what we could've done better."

I nodded. What could I say? She had to live with her memories and I with mine. I felt no antipathy for this old woman and didn't sense any from her, either.

A couple of days later, Claudia, Marco, Julia, and Liliana took me out to see beautiful Copacabana and all the other beaches around Rio. After that, we visited the Pao de Acucar (Sugar Loaf Mountain), where we rode to its summit in a cable car. I was doing the tourist bit and they were very happy to show me their world. Rio de Janeiro is one of the most stunning cities I have ever visited and when I looked down at it from the peak of the mountain, its beauty was breathtaking.

I stared in awe at the Cristo Redentor—the statue of Christ the Redeemer—one of the world's most recognized monuments.

Looking out through the windows as we rode the electric train up Corcovado Mountain, I felt dizzy as I took in the spectacular Cidade Maravilhosa—Marvellous City—below.

Doing all these things with my new family made everything very thrilling and the get-togethers with my brother's family were frequent and happy. I was told that the family was never very close but I reunited them by bringing them together. Apparently, my brother and his mom had not spoken in a long time but now, the mother-son love clearly showed.

One morning, I asked Claudia if I could look at her pictures. I wanted to see what they had looked like growing up and I wanted to see pictures of my father. It was an adventure, looking at these family photos. Through my brother's wedding pictures as well as my sister's, I saw them as a family, happy, no worries.

"Would you take me to see his grave?" I asked Claudia.

"Of course, we'll go tomorrow. I had thought about asking if you wanted to go, but wasn't sure how you'd react."

The next morning after breakfast, Dona Matilda, Claudia and I, got ready to go to the cemetery.

My father's grave was at the top of a hill and as we got out of the car, I held my half-sister's hand for comfort, feeling a knot form in my throat. She guided me to the site where I knelt on the grass and touched the cold marble of my father's grave. I swept aside a few grains of soil with my fingers, and his name became visible.

Eduardo Afonso
* 22-03-1912
+ 27-08-1979

My thoughts emptied onto that gravestone all the longing and regret I'd held for decades.

> Hello, Father. I know you
> never thought I'd make it this far
> but here I am. Running away
> from me didn't really accomplish
> much, did it? By doing that you
> caused me a lot of pain. I've
> gotten over it and I want you to
> know that I forgive you, but I
> just wanted to see what kind of
> man does what you did to me
> and my mother. Too bad you are
> dead and will never get to see
> that I did well, in spite of all the
> odds against me.
> I often wondered if you
> ever thought of me. Did you?
> Did you ever think of your baby

girl who would've loved to have

called you Daddy?

I hoped my thoughts transmitted themselves to him, wherever he was. Nonetheless, I wanted him to rest in peace.

I stood. My sister came to me, ready to embrace me. We held each other and the tears finally came. We sobbed in each other's arms.

I had found him. My search was over.

The day before I left, Dona Matilda came to me with a small box in her hands. She looked at me kindly and handed it to me.

"Just a small token, so you can remember me, my daughter."

Inside the box was a beautiful purple natural stone necklace and matching earrings. My vision blurred as I bent to kiss and hug her.

At the airport the next day, I said so long to all of them and then blew them all a kiss before the airport engulfed me.

Chapter Twenty-Eight

A Path to Forgiveness

Now that I'd found my father, that part of my story was somewhat clear. But I would've liked to have faced him and asked him why he'd never looked for me or if he'd ever had a thought whether I was dead or still alive. What made him think he could just father a child, then leave that child to fend for herself? Did he have any regrets when he met his maker?

Earlier in the year, I'd torn my rotator cuff and after much pain and many visits to different doctors, I learned I had to have surgery. It was my right arm, so using my left arm to run my everyday life was going to be challenging.

At the time, my Aunt Licinia, who had always been and was still a very dear part of my life, lived in Newmarket, close to where we'd once lived. I phoned and asked if she'd come up and stay for a while, helping me out until I had control of my arm again.

"I'm sorry, I can't do that," she replied.

"Why not? I need you. What's up?"

"I'm going to visit my daughter and her husband. Ever since I moved out of Kingston, I never get to see Sabrina and Zackary anymore. I would really like to come and see you," she said, "but unfortunately, I won't be there when you need me. I'm sorry."

I wanted to spend some time with my aunt, so I didn't give up. "I have to go for pre-op this week. Want to come up then? I could pick you up on my way from Toronto."

"Sure. That'd be great," my aunt said. "I'll be waiting for you with my bags packed."

I laughed. "You can help me prepare for my journey into the operating room."

"How did you manage to tear your shoulder up, anyway?" she asked.

"I'm not sure, really, but I suspect I did it when I was carrying my desktop to the local computer repair man and I tripped on the sidewalk."

"Tripped over what?"

"I guess I stepped at the edge of the sidewalk and went flying. I saved the computer, but my shoulder hit the side of the building and got hurt."

"Getting clumsy in your old age?" she teased.

"Look who's talking. You fell last year, and dislocated your shoulder as well."

"Yes, but I'm an old woman of almost eighty. My balance isn't what it used to be."

"All right then," I said. "Let's get together, drink some Merlot, and celebrate aging gracefully."

"I like your way of thinking. I'll go to the liquor store and make sure we have enough."

It has been said that you don't have to like the family you're born to, and that you can pick your own. Given the choice, I would always pick my aunt.

The day of my pre-op I called my aunt before I left home.

"Instead of picking you up on the way from Toronto, would you like to come to the doctor with me?" I asked.

"Of course, I would."

I left home at nine that morning and the air was crisp but not yet cold. I climbed into my vehicle, turned on my audio book and set off on the two-hour drive to Newmarket.

There isn't much in the way of civilization along the way, but there is a lot of nature to admire. The country roads in this part of the country are glorious in autumn. My eyes feasted on the spectacle of the trees wearing their array of brilliant fall colours. It's not uncommon to see deer, fox, and the odd chipmunk or squirrel, scampering to the side of the road ahead of the car. I've even seen wild turkeys in the fields.

In spring, when life emerges again, one of the greatest joys of living in the country is witnessing the mama birds train their young, flying beneath them to ensure they have a place to rest, should their tiny wings get tired.

When I arrived at my aunt's building, she was waiting for me inside the glass door, as promised.

"So, what's the plan?" she asked.

"I'm going to see the surgeon."

"And then?" She looked at me from the corner of her eye, a naughty smile playing on her lips.

I grinned. "We'll go to lunch," I said as I pulled out of the parking lot.

"That's my girl."

Once we'd driven out of Newmarket and were on our way into the city, my aunt cleared her throat.

"I phoned your mother last week," she said.

A wave of guilt washed over me. I could go months, sometimes a year or two, before I called my mother. I write to her every Christmas but when I call, I never really know what to say to her. So, I don't call.

"And, how is she?" I asked.

"She's not well at all. Not bad considering she has advanced diabetes, but her disposition hasn't improved."

"Why am I not surprised?"

My aunt sighed with resignation. "Just as your mother was telling me how everything was fine, that nothing had changed, your stepfather picked up the other line. He sounded furious."

She frowned and lowered her voice, pretending to be my step father.

"'Licinia," he said to me, "don't be surprised if you don't see me when you come to Portugal again. Angelina is driving me crazy and I will be divorcing her soon. She's stubborn, she doesn't do what she's told and she calls me names all the time. I've had enough."

Tia Licinia shook her head sadly. "I tried to calm him down but he was so upset he wouldn't let me get a word in. Then the phone went dead. I just sat there, staring at the phone, amazed by what had just transpired."

"You don't really think they're getting a divorce, do you?"

She shrugged. "He certainly sounded serious. I can't understand how a woman who's practically blind from diabetes can be so unkind and thoughtless towards a man who's been taking care of her for so long. It doesn't make sense."

"Did you say he complained that she doesn't do what she's told?"

"Yes, can you believe that?"

"Auntie, when I'm eighty years old, I probably won't do what I'm told, either. He shouldn't be telling her what to do, just help her when she needs it. My stepfather was always bossy."

She took a deep breath then blew it out again. "You're right, I guess. But it won't do her any good if he leaves her. Then what will happen to her?"

"You know, all her life she's taken care of him. I think it's time he took care of her, don't you?" I asked.

"He's not thinking that way. All he thinks about is how she behaves now and it doesn't sound good."

"That's the problem. It's sad." I said.

"What's sad?" my aunt questioned.

"There's no justice here. I lived with them for close to ten years and I know both of them well. My stepfather thinks he's the boss and I think deep down she resents him for all he's put her through. She spent her life trying to please him, never getting much in return."

"Your mother isn't the ideal roommate either."

"No, she's not, but can you imagine living a life without tenderness? Without hearing your man say "I love you?""

"I know very well how that is," she said with a weary smile.

"Sorry, Tia. I know everyone has their moments, but I have never seen my stepfather look at my mother with anything but cool superiority."

"I don't know," my aunt said, sounding sceptical. "It's a little late in their lives to be thinking of personalities. All I know is it won't do your mother any good if he decides to leave her."

"Well, I certainly can't move to Portugal to take care of her, but she has two other children, certainly either my half-brother or sister will take care of her."

"Look, your mother is practically blind and she has bad legs. Your sister lives on the second floor of that old building and your mother would never be able to negotiate all those stairs. She would either have a heart attack on the way up or fall and kill herself on the way down. I just don't see it happening."

At the restaurant, Aunt Licinia sat back and took a sip of her wine. "Lourdes, I'm going to Portugal next March with Sabrina and Zachary. I still have some money invested there and sometimes I could really use it. I want my money here and I want to have access to it without having to fly over the Atlantic."

Something stirred within me as I heard these words. After finding out about my father, most of the uneasiness about him had lifted, but I thought there was more I needed to do in order for my soul to have peace.

"Tia, would you mind if I came to Portugal with you?

She glanced at me, hopeful. "Why would I mind? I would love it."

"The only thing is, I can't go in March, Dan and I will be in Florida."

"So, when are you thinking of going?" she asked.

"August."

"Can I come with you when you go?"

My aunt surprised me once more. "Where? To Portugal? I thought you said you were all going in March?"

"So, I'll go again. You know I love going there with you. Besides, Sabrina won't go to see your mother because of the way she was treated last time she was there, but I can't go over and not see her."

"Great," I said. "We'll both go to Portugal in August."

She nodded, satisfied. "It's settled then. Can I ask why you're going to Portugal?"

I hadn't been prepared for that question. My aunt kept looking at me, waiting for an answer and suddenly I had trouble finding the words.

"I'm going because …" I faltered, then dove right in. "I want to see my mother one more time while she's still alive. I want to make things right between us, you know? I have long ago forgiven her for the treatment I received in her house and as far as I'm concerned, everything is forgiven and right. But I would like to have just a few words with her so I could tell her exactly that. And maybe I'll get that hug I've waited for all my life." I shrugged. "I don't know. Maybe it's just a silly dream but the older I get, the more I want to make things right. Do you know what I'm talking about?"

"I do."

Flying over the Atlantic to Portugal is a long and tiring flight. It is just over seven hours, but it's the time change that really messes me up. My aunt and I left Toronto at 6:00 pm and we arrived in Lisbon at 6:00 the next morning.

I phoned my stepfather that evening and he said he wanted to see me so he could explain why he was going to leave my mother. I had barely hung up with him when my phone rang again and it was Paulo, saying he wanted to see us that evening. I was excited and happy when Paulo met us shortly after eight in the hotel lobby. He was now forty-two years old but his wife, Sonia, didn't look a day older than the last time I'd seen her. My godson, Fabio, was a terrific sixteen-year-old boy with excellent manners and their chatty ten-year-old daughter, Inez, kept us all amused. Paulo drove us to Cascais where we enjoyed a meal, talked about old times, and caught up on recent happenings.

"I didn't call Ana to join us because lately she doesn't get along with anyone, mainly my father and me."

"What's her problem—why is she so resentful?" I asked.

"Not sure. I just know that every time we all get together, there's always a fight at some point. My father doesn't care much for her either but I feel sorry for Mom, she is sort of in the middle of it all. She has not been well. She had a small stroke a little while ago and is very fragile right now. It would be nice if Ana was a little more supportive of her but mainly, I think she would be happier if we all got along."

"Have you tried talking with her?"

Paulo gave me a sideways look that clearly said, 'Are you kidding? I couldn't be bothered.'

I didn't know what to say. There was obviously a lot of anger and mistrust here, so I said nothing.

"Did my father say he wanted to see you?" Paulo asked.

"Yes, although I don't know why it would matter what I think. This is a family matter and I haven't been part of this family for a very long time, don't know why he wants to see me."

"I'll come with you," he offered, "I'll drive you to them."

The next day, we didn't meet my mother and stepfather at their house, my aunt and I met them at a park. My mother sat alone on a bench and my stepfather paced back and forth, not far from where she waited. As we approached, my mother stood up and embraced me with her thin arms and my stepfather stood to one side, an annoyed expression on his face.

"See how nice she is to you?" he challenged, "She's not that nice all the time. Every time I tell her something, she always ignores me and calls me names."

"How are you, Mom, how are you feeling?" I asked, trying to stay neutral. My mother did not look well at all.

But as soon as my mother released me from her embrace, it was like a nightmare. They turned to each other and while he told her he was tired of putting up with her, she retorted by saying she was tired of him as well, why didn't he leave her alone and go to hell.

I covered my ears while at the same time I wanted to save my mother from all this upset, this was so embarrassing. Paulo just stayed off to one side and after a while I joined him. My aunt tried to placate my mother but it wasn't helping.

Finally, I had enough. I walked over to them and put my hands up. "Listen up everyone, I didn't come all the way from Canada to hear you fight. I think you've done enough of that all your lives. Let's go, finish this. I will take you all to lunch and we'll pretend this never happened. Do you agree?

They both calmed down and looked at me and finally, they both nodded their heads while inside mine, a horrible ache started.

The next day, Paulo and his family picked us up and we met my mother and stepfather for lunch again. A mere shell of her old self, my mother appeared so sad and broken. She had to look where she was going and she moved so very slowly. She looked even worse than she did the day before, if that was possible. My heart broke when I hugged her and her bony arms clung to me as if she didn't want to let me go. As we walked through a mall to find a restaurant, she hung on to my arm for support and took careful, slow steps. She was blind in one eye and the other one was weak. I gently guided her through the mall, looking for a store to buy her a pair of comfortable shoes. Her swollen feet made her shoes too tight. I questioned her about that and she admitted that her feet were sore.

We finally came across a shoe store and I insisted we stop so I could shop for her. I ended up buying her a pair of soft leather shoes she said felt as if her feet were wrapped in cotton.

We had lunch but my mother hardly ate anything and seemed to be on the verge of tears all the time. When we finally said goodbye at the hotel, she hugged me again and told me how wonderful I made her feel.

I could hardly sleep that night. My mind kept returning to earlier in the day and watching my mother behave so vulnerable and sad. I couldn't help but imagine her existing in this state—old, uncared for, and unhappy. Images of her kept running through my mind.

God, have mercy on her, I prayed. I realized I had never seen her happy, with the exception of so long ago when we met the man in the suit at the coffee shop and when she played with Paulo or Ana. I watched people interact with her, including her own family, but I never noticed much compassion in their interaction with her. My stepfather may have loved her in his own way, but he walked in front of her and expected her to keep up, which was very hard for her to do. The image of her following him to the car was still fresh in my mind and it broke my heart to think about it. I realized tears were soaking my pillow and had to will myself to stop. It was out of my control.

The next day, my stepfather brought my mother to meet us again but before they got there, my aunt and I went to a store and bought her some outfits. We had lunch again and she seemed almost happy. When I told her that I was planning on taking her to Fatima, the holy place where the Virgin appeared to the three shepherd children, she didn't get excited but she agreed to go.

Just the three of us. My mother, my aunt and I.

When her husband brought her the next morning, I led her into our hotel room and right into the bathroom.

I helped my mother undress, then I got into the tub with her while my aunt got the clothes together. With tender care I washed her hair, then handed her the soap to wash herself. Afterwards, I dried her hair, curled it, and introduced her to her new clothes. She was shocked and couldn't stop telling me what a wonderful daughter I was, thanking me for all this.

At ten in the morning we met the bus that would take us to Fatima. My mother looked comfortable and presentable in her new clothes and shoes. She limped beside us due to pain in her hips and knees so I took her arm and helped her along.

When we arrived in Fatima, we were told we had four hours in which to enjoy the sites. It took us a while to reach the basilica because the driver parked the bus far away and my mother walked very slowly, but we still had plenty of time.

Mass was being celebrated and I asked my mother if she'd like to attend. I told her she didn't have to take part in communion if she didn't want to, all she'd have to do was cross her arms over her chest when the time came, and she'd be given a blessing, instead.

She shook her head weakly. "It's been so long since I've been in a church, I wouldn't know what to do."

"Then don't do anything," I said. "Just be there. God will take care of the rest."

She followed meekly as I guided her inside. The congregation filled every seat. My mother was too weak to stand for long but fortunately, some people saw us coming in and made room for us in the first pew. I was grateful.

Not long after we sat down, everyone stood for "Our Father." My mother remained seated as she didn't know you were to stand up for that prayer but when I looked down, I could see that her palms were together and her head bowed, as she prayed. A tear slid down my cheek as I watched my mother make her peace with God.

We followed everyone for communion and I didn't have to repeat myself. My mother crossed her arms over her chest and walked in front of me. As she approached the celebrant, I was astonished to see a wafer being placed on her tongue, instead of just a blessing. Later, she asked me why she'd been given communion when all she'd wanted was a blessing.

"It was meant to be, Mom, be happy for it. God loves you."

At the end of the day, the bus left us a little distance from the hotel and I held onto my mother as she shuffled along beside me. It had been a long day for her. When we reached the hotel, my stepfather was waiting for us, an annoyed expression on his face.

"Did she behave?" he asked, pointing at my mother.

"Yes, she did. She was wonderful," I said.

"I will take her home, have a good flight back," he said as he began to turn away. I hugged my mother goodbye, wondering if I would ever see her again. A lot of emotions rose up as I closed my eyes and hugged her tight, wanting to feel her essence flow into me, wanting to feel the love I had yearned for, wanting to feel my mother.

When I realized she was sobbing in my arms, I could no longer keep it together and I sobbed with her. Such pain and relief in my heart. I finally felt my mother, her love for me, we were one, mother and child.

There is no greater love, after all.

She pulled back and looked into my eyes through hers, flooded with tears. "My beautiful daughter, will you ever forgive me, for everything?"

I sobbed as I looked at this woman who gave birth to me and then abandoned me. I looked at this woman and, at last, saw my mother. I was a child again, I wanted to be loved and then realized I **was** loved, by my mother. There were no words to express my joy.

I hugged her tight and whispered, "I forgive you, Mom."

Epilogue

June is the month of my mother's birth. In 2012, a week before she turned eighty- two, my mother went shopping with her husband and, on the way to the car, she fell. The next day she sat outside their little house on the beach and she just collapsed to the side, unconscious. An ambulance was called and she was taken to hospital. Later that day, she was transported to a nursing home, just outside Lisbon.

Ana emailed me and so did Paulo. I don't know why they still didn't get along, they barely communicated with each other but both their messages were very clear.

My mother had suffered a stroke.

Dan didn't object when I told him I had to go to Portugal to see my mother immediately. After calling my aunt and telling her my plans, I called for airplane tickets and we both flew to Portugal the next day. I had no issues left with my mother but I wanted to see her one more time—just one more time.

As we arrived at the home, the attending physician spoke with us before she led us to my mother's room, cautioning us about her fragility and warning not to show a lot of emotion as she didn't want her patient agitated. We were supposed to be cheerful and happy, but I didn't know how I'd manage that.

I took my mother's hand and tried to sound cheerful.

"Ola, Mae." I said tentatively. "It's me, Lourdes. Do you remember me?"

A weak "Yes."

I leaned in close to her face and asked if I could have a kiss. Her lips caressed my cheek and I closed my eyes as she made kissing sounds.

My aunt and I stayed for a week and my mother stabilized. I left Portugal wondering if she even realized we had been there.

Her husband also had a stroke a week after they institutionalized my mother. He was taken to a home where he had to be restrained because he didn't want to stay, he kept saying he wanted to go home to his wife. His feelings for her must've run deep, although he didn't express them very well. This man lived a rough life with no direction, ambition or flare. Although he was born and raised in Lisbon, he wasn't much different than the people raised in the unrefined villages of the north. Two weeks later, he refused to eat and when they tried to feed him intravenously, he ripped the tube off his arm. He eventually died, a month after they took my mother away from him.

On May 23, 2013, I received the fateful email. My mother had passed away. I never thought her death would affect me the way it did. I cried for days. I could not find a way to overcome my sadness, my loss.

My heart broke again when my beloved Tia Licinia passed away in 2020 at the age of eighty-six. It had nothing to do with the COVID-19 pandemic that brought the entire globe to its knees. I think she died of loneliness in the institution she lived in. My cousin Sabrina took care of her and visited often. I visited her as well and took her out to dinner every time I saw her, but I lived far away and could not visit her more than once or sometimes twice a month. She still loved her wine and so I made sure she had money to go to the bar in the home every day and have a glass of wine. It made me happy to do that for her and it made her happy as well. A daily blessing in her otherwise isolated life.

With her passing, Sabrina and I became closer than ever and, together, we made sure her mother left this world with all the dignity she deserved. We shared our grief and mourned a soul who was beloved by both of us. I hope to encounter my Tia again someday, in some other dimension.

When I think of the people who assured my survival up until I could take care of myself, I can only give true credit to two. My grandmother, who sacrificed everything so that I may grow up to be a respectful and loving person who appreciates what she has and never takes anything or anyone for granted. She taught me all that in the short formative years I had with her.

My stepfather, my padrinho. His silent presence in my life was like an angel's. I remember him defending me once, but now I think he was always there, looking out for me and my survival. It's a little late, but I want to thank these two angels in my life. I want to acknowledge their kindness and their protection, and I want them to know that I will be forever grateful.

As for the others who hurt me deeply and caused my life to be so painful, it took much of my adult life to understand what it means to forgive someone. I knew I should learn it but I found it very hard to understand how I could possibly forgive someone who had caused me so much harm. After a lot of soul searching, I realized that forgiveness was not about excusing their behaviour, it was about letting go so my soul would be free of bitterness.

I'm forever grateful for all I have accomplished. I have a family, peace of mind and a lot of love in my life. These are the things I so fervently prayed for in the little bedroom of my mother's home and later on when I came to Canada but my life was still a prisoner to others.

Despite the shame and abuse of my early years, all that I wished for was granted to me. Indeed, I feel blessed.

Now that I'm in the autumn of my life, these thoughts surface without any prompting or any answers.

I do believe I turned out all right. If someone needs money and I have it, I give them money. If someone needs clothing, I give them what I have. If someone needs a shoulder, I'm there. If I go to a restaurant and see someone who needs a meal, I buy it for them. I would not hesitate to give all I have and I always smile at an old comment from my husband.

"If you have a hundred dollars, it won't last long in your wallet because you will give it away."

I'm proud of who I am and I think I turned out to be a good person, after all.

"Every tear is a word that needs to be written"... Paulo Coelho

Acknowledgements

There are too many people who directly or indirectly contributed to the writing of this memoir to mention each by name. Know that I am grateful for your support and contributions even if you are not specifically thanked below. It truly took a village … as the saying goes.

I'd like to acknowledge my friend, Tulia Ferreira, who was the first person to get a glimpse of what this memoir was all about. Her friendship and inspiration are what made me want to write this book.

I have to thank my dashing husband, Dan, for the patience he showed when I spent hours in the basement, at my desk, reliving and recording the passage of years that put this story together. I must say that his supper was never late and I still managed to be the attentive wife.

I would like to thank my friends Kathy Kelly and Dolores Adams for their encouragement to bring this work to fruition and last but not in any way least, I send my gratitude to Ruth Walker and Marie Gage, who helped me make this a reality.

Author's Note

To finally tell my story has been a dream come true. After living a life of nightmares and wondering what people would think about me if they knew the real story, is now a thing of the past. By telling my story I liberated my soul and hopefully, the people who care about me will take this as a lesson in their own lives and not criticize what I could've done to make my life better. It's been a journey, trust me.

I managed to live my life with the idea that I couldn't change the past and therefore I must acknowledge the lessons it taught me. One of the most powerful was the fact that I now understand that all this was meant for the advancement of my soul. Perhaps I needed to learn what it was like to be defenseless, to learn to love with every fiber of my being in spite of it all, to bring awareness to parents that their child may be being abused without their knowledge, or to help people (including myself) feel gratitude for all they have in their lives.

About the Author
Maria Trautman

Maria Lives in the beautiful Haliburton Highlands, Ontario, Canada with her husband Dan.

She enjoys journaling, gardening, Tai Chi, Golf and enjoying the company of her children and Grandchildren. When asked what prompted her to write this book, her answer is:

"To free my soul."

I would love to connect with you so feel free to visit Author Maria Trautman on Facebook.

Made in the USA
Las Vegas, NV
11 September 2023

77412468R00174